Advanced Information and Knowledge Processing

Series editors

Lakhmi C. Jain
Bournemouth University, Poole, UK and
University of South Australia, Adelaide, Australia

Xindong Wu
University of Vermont

Information systems and intelligent knowledge processing are playing an increasing role in business, science and technology. Recently, advanced information systems have evolved to facilitate the co-evolution of human and information networks within communities. These advanced information systems use various paradigms including artificial intelligence, knowledge management, and neural science as well as conventional information processing paradigms. The aim of this series is to publish books on new designs and applications of advanced information and knowledge processing paradigms in areas including but not limited to aviation, business, security, education, engineering, health, management, and science. Books in the series should have a strong focus on information processing—preferably combined with, or extended by, new results from adjacent sciences. Proposals for research monographs, reference books, coherently integrated multi-author edited books, and handbooks will be considered for the series and each proposal will be reviewed by the Series Editors, with additional reviews from the editorial board and independent reviewers where appropriate. Titles published within the Advanced Information and Knowledge Processing series are included in Thomson Reuters' Book Citation Index.

More information about this series at http://www.springer.com/series/4738

Mohammed Zuhair Al-Taie • Seifedine Kadry

Python for Graph and Network Analysis

 Springer

Mohammed Zuhair Al-Taie
Faculty of Computing
Universiti Teknologi Malaysia
Kuala Lumpur, Malaysia

Seifedine Kadry
School of Engineering and Technology
American University of the Middle East
Kuwait

ISSN 1610-3947   ISSN 2197-8441   (electronic)
Advanced Information and Knowledge Processing
ISBN 978-3-319-85037-5   ISBN 978-3-319-53004-8   (eBook)
DOI 10.1007/978-3-319-53004-8

Printed on acid-free paper

This Springer imprint is published by Springer Nature
The registered company is Springer International Publishing AG
The registered company address is: Gewerbestrasse 11, 6330 Cham, Switzerland

Preface

New Age of Web Usage

The fast developments in the Web and Internet in the last decade and the advancements in computing and communication have drawn people in innovative ways. Huge participatory social sites have emerged, empowering new shapes of collaboration communication. Sites, such as Twitter, Facebook, LinkedIn, and Myspace, allow people to make new virtual relationships. Wikis, blogs, and video blogs provide users with convenience and assistance in every possible way to help them publish their ideas and thoughts, no need to worry about publishing costs. A tremendous number of volunteers can today write articles and share photos, videos, and links at a scope and scale never imagined before. Product recommendations provided by online marketplaces such as eBay and Amazon (after analyzing user behavior) can tempt online consumers to make more orders. Tagging mechanisms on the Web help users to express their preferences. Sending and receiving e-mails, visiting a Webpage, or posting a comment on a blog site leaves a digital footprint that can be traced back to the person or group behind it. Political movements can also use the Web today to create new forms of collaboration between supporters.

All these changes would not have taken place without the help of Web 2.0 technology—a term coined by Tim O'Reilly to show that Internet users are more prepared than before to reformulate the Web content.

Social networking is a major factor in the emergence of such interactions since most Internet users are players of social sites and use them regularly and actively.

Recent studies have shown that social networking has become one of three popular uses of the Internet, alongside the Internet search and e-mail, which points to the importance of this social trend and the role it plays in communities.

In the study of social networks, social network analysis makes an interesting interdisciplinary research area, where computer scientists and sociologists bring their competence to a level that will enable them to meet the challenges of this fast-developing field. Computer scientists have the knowledge to parse and process data, while sociologists have the experience that is required for efficient data editing and interpretation.

Social network analysis techniques, which are included in this book, will help readers to efficiently analyze social data from Twitter, Facebook, LiveJournal, GitHub, and many others at three levels of depth: ego, group, and community. They will be able to analyze militant and revolutionary networks and candidate networks during elections. They will even learn how the Ebola virus spread through communities.

Social network analysis was successfully applied in different fields such as health, cyber security, business, animal social networks, information retrieval, and communications. For example, in animal social networks, social network analysis was used to investigate relationships and social structures of animal gatherings and the direct and indirect interactions between animal groups. It was also applied by security agencies, particularly after the 9/11/2001 attacks, to study the structure and dynamics of militant groups.

Learn, in Simple Words, Theory and Practice of Social Network Analysis

This is a book on graph and network analysis integrating theory and applications for performing the analysis. Step by step, the book introduces the main structural concepts and their applications in social research. It is aimed at tackling problems on graphs and social networks by exploring tens of examples ranging in difficulty from simple to intermediate, which makes the book a practical introduction to the field.

In each of the eight chapters (except for chapter one), each theoretical section is followed by examples explaining how to perform graph and network analysis with Python, a general-purpose programming language that is becoming more and more popular to do data science. Companies worldwide are using Python to harvest insights from their data and get a competitive edge. The book also includes the use of NetworkX library, a Python language software package and an open-source tool for the creation, manipulation, and study of the structure, dynamics, and functions of complex networks. Side by side with Matplotlib package for data visualization, these three open source tools are used to analyze and visualize social data. In the end, the reader has the knowledge, skills, and tools to apply social network analysis in all reachable fields, ranging from social media to business administration and history.

The book is intended for readers who want to learn theory and practice of graph and network analysis using a programming language, which is Python, without going too far into its mathematical or statistical methods. In fact, the book is suitable for courses on social network analysis in all disciplines that use social methodology. We believe that many of the readers are more interested in the implementation of social network analysis than in its mathematical properties.

The book contains eight chapters. Chapter 1: Theoretical Concepts of Network Analysis. This is the longest chapter, it gives an introduction to the major theoretical concepts of network analysis, with emphasis on these used throughout this book.

Chapter 2: Graph theory. This chapter presents the main features of graph theory, the mathematical study of the application and properties of graphs, initially motivated by the study of games of chance. It addresses topics such as origins of graph theory, graph basics, types of graphs, graph traversals, and types of operations on graphs.

Chapter 3: Network basics. This chapter introduces the concept of a network, which is, of course, the core object of network analysis. We will discuss topics such as types of networks, network measures, installation and use of NetworkX library, network data representation, basic matrix operations, and data visualization.

Chapter 4: Social networks. This chapter introduces the main concepts of social networks such as properties of social networks, data collection in social networks, data sampling, and social network analysis.

Chapter 5: Node-level analysis. This chapter is concerned with building an understanding of how to do network analysis at the node (ego) level. It shows how to create social networks from scratch, how to import networks, how to find key players in social networks using centrality measures, and how to visualize networks. We will also introduce the important algorithms that are used to gain insights from graphs.

Chapter 6: Group-level analysis. In this chapter, we are going to present a number of techniques for detecting cohesive groups in networks such as cliques, clustering coefficient, triadic analysis, structural holes, brokerage, transitivity, hierarchical clustering, and blockmodels, all of which are based on how nodes in a network interconnect. However, among all, cohesion and brokerage types of analysis are two major research topics in social network analysis.

Chapter 7: Network-level analysis. In this chapter, we are going to study graphs and networks as a whole, which is different from what we have done in the previous chapters when we analyzed graphs at the node level and the group level. Hence, this chapter addresses concepts such as components and isolates, cores and periphery, network density, shortest paths, reciprocity, affiliation networks and two-mode networks, and homophily.

Chapter 8: Information diffusion in social networks. This chapter discusses concepts of information diffusion in social networks. Information diffusion methods are commonly used in viral marketing, in collaborative filtering systems, in emergency management, in community detection, and in the study of citation networks.

Johor, Malaysia   Mohammed Zuhair Al-Taie
Egaila, Kuwait   Seifedine Kadry

Contents

Chapter 1
Theoretical Concepts of Network Analysis

Generally speaking, a network is a set of links (ties or edges) and objects (nodes or vertices). These objects could be people, rivers, roads, computers, cities, etc., while links may represent relationships such as friendship, kinship, sexual relationships, the flow of information, etc. Kinds of networks include computer networks, neural networks, semantic networks, food web, supply chain networks, friendship networks, information networks, etc. Network representation borrows some of its notations (e.g., nodes and links) from graph theory and other notations (e.g., the actor-network theory) from social theories.

A network can be represented as a graph or matrix to show connections between nodes. This allows applying a variety of mathematical, computational, and statistical techniques to extract and analyze the main features of the network.

This chapter gives an introduction to the major theoretical concepts of network analysis, with emphasis on these used throughout this book. It is not meant to provide a comprehensive list of the topics that are included in graph and network analysis as the topic is incredibly rich.

1.1 Sociological Meaning of Network Relations

Sociologically, a network is a set of relations between actors. Actors can mean individuals, groups, organizations, states, etc. Actors in a network may or may not have relationships with each other. Relations between nodes in a network are called ties. A tie can have several meanings. For example, it can mean kinship with people, affection, enmity, exchange of favors or loans, membership in a club, or attending certain events together. Ties can have direction. Relationships such as knowing, kinship, or shared membership in organizations are usually directionless, but ties of authorship usually have direction.

Social networks are theoretical models to analyze and visualize the relations between actors. Relations between individuals may vary in intensity, such that some

© Springer International Publishing AG 2017   1
M.Z. Al-Taie, S. Kadry, *Python for Graph and Network Analysis*, Advanced
Information and Knowledge Processing, DOI 10.1007/978-3-319-53004-8_1

ties are stronger than others. It is also possible to have more than one kind of relation among individuals in a network. For example, a group of students in a college may be connected to each other through friendship, common courses, club memberships, etc., where each of these relations is different from the others.

Another important concept that is related to relations among actors within social networks is transitivity: suppose that we know that actor a knows actor b and actor b knows actor c. Does that also imply that actor a also knows actor c?

The relational structure of a social network can be represented as a graph of nodes $N = \{1,,2,,3...n\}$, where each pair of nodes is connected by an edge. The graph can also be represented as an adjacency matrix X in which $\{X_{ij}\}$ is the relationship between node i (sender) and node j (receiver). $\{X_{ij}\}$ can take a binary value either 1 or 0 indicating the presence or absence of the relationship between i and j.

Since actors in a social network are likely to be related to each other based on age, sex, religion, language, education, etc., it is possible to cluster these actors based on a given similarity measure. This has several implications. For example, organizations can use the clustering of users into groups to develop a different product for each group of consumers. It also allows finding key players and influential users who are likely to be influential in their local social circles. Let's consider the following different types of social networks in which the type of relationships between actors is different from one network to another.

- In most online social networks (e.g., Facebook), most relations are a type of friendship (a mutual relation) between two friends. We can represent the relations in this case as a directed edge with two heads or as an undirected edge if we want to show logical equivalence.
- In some other networks (e.g., Twitter), relations are a type of "follow" model (which are not necessarily mutual) which means that an actor a can follow actors $b, c, d, ...$, but it is not necessary that these actors also follow actor a. A relationship of this type is represented as an edge with one head.
- A social communication network is a type of social networks in which nodes are some service users (e.g., phone users) and relationships (edges) correspond to a communication between two users who were present at the same event (i.e., talk). These networks can also be thought of as a type of "social graphs" as they allow for various types of social relations to be represented as a graph depicting communication or friendship networks. Such a graph would allow connecting users and distributing their content, and the strength of a relationship between two users, in this case, can be set as the number of talks attended by both participants.
- Trust networks are also another type of social graphs in which the relationship between two entities allows one entity (trustor) to rely on (trust) the actions performed by the other entity (trustee). These entities can be two persons, one person, and an object, or groups of families, companies, countries, etc.
- In citation networks, an arrow can be used to describe a citation relationship from actor a who cited actor b.

• In the blogosphere, a relation can be established between actor *a* and actor *b* if the latter commented on a post published by the former.

A social network can contain millions of users. Some of these users are more active or more powerful than other users. In order to distinguish between the different users in a social network, a number of network measurements such as degree, closeness, betweenness, and eigenvector centralities were developed. These measurements can extract, based on a defined criterion, the users who are more important than others. Degree centrality, for example, considers the number of direct links to other users as the measure of importance. Closeness centrality measures how close a user is to the other users in the network. Betweenness centrality describes how important a user is as a link between different network segments. Eigenvector centrality defines the important user as the one who is connected to important users in the network.

1.2 Network Measurements

A number of measurable network characteristics were developed to gain a greater insight into networks, with many of them having their roots in social studies on the relationships among social actors. In this section, we will discuss three categories of measurements that have been defined in the social network analysis stream:

1. Network connection, which includes transitivity, multiplexity, homophily, dyads and mutuality, balance and triads, and reciprocity
2. Network distribution, which includes the distance between nodes, degree centrality, closeness centrality, betweenness centrality, eigenvector centrality, PageRank, geodesic distance and shortest path, eccentricity, and density
3. Network segmentation, which includes cohesive subgroups, cliques, clustering coefficient, k-cores, core/periphery, blockmodels, and hierarchical clustering

1.2.1 Network Connection

Network connection (or connectivity) refers to the ability to move from one node to another in a network. It is the ratio between route distance and geodesic distance. Connectivity can be calculated locally (for a part of the network) and globally (for the entire network). Let's take a look at some of the important metrics of network connection.

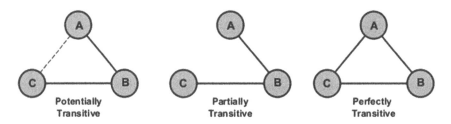

Fig. 1.1 Transitivity between nodes

1.2.2 Transitivity

Transitivity is a network property that refers to the extent to which a relation between two nodes is transitive. It is a very important measure in social networks but less important in other types of networks. In social networks, the term transitivity reflects the friend-of-a-friend concept. It is sometimes used as a synonym of whole-network clustering coefficient.

Suppose that we have an actor *A* who is connected through an edge to actor *B* and *B* is connected to actor *C*. Does that meant that *A* is also connected to *C*? (Fig. 1.1).

An answer with "yes" to this question implies that the triad (a subgraph formed by three nodes) shows an ideal transitive relationship. If "no," then the triad lacks a cohesive relationship among its nodes. The average transitivity of a social network is defined as the number of triangles over the number of connected triples.

$$Transitiviy = \frac{3 * No.\ of\ triangles}{No.\ connected\ triples}$$

where the multiplier 3 accounts for the fact that each triangle contributes to three different connected triples in the graph, one centered at each node. A value of 1 means that the network contains all possible edges. In real social networks, a value between 0.3 and 0.6 is common for the transitivity index.

The transitivity of a graph is strongly related to the clustering coefficient (a measure of how much nodes tend to form dense subgraphs) as each of them measures the relative frequency of triangles. They are the most common measures used to calculate the number of triangles in a network.

1.2.3 Multiplexity

Ties can have strength. This can be in the form of the intensity of the relationship or by how many different types of content that the tie contains. Ties with only one dimension are called "uniplex," while ties with more than one dimension are called "multiplex." Typically, multiplex ties are stronger than uniplex ties. Nodes and ties

Fig. 1.2 Simple
sociogram

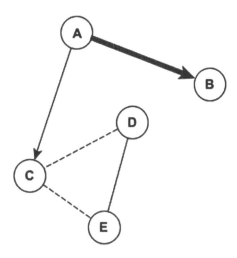

Table 1.1 Matrix representation of the sociogram

	A	B	C	D	E
A	0	1	1	0	0
B	0	0	0	0	0
C	0	0	0	1	1
D	0	0	1	0	1
E	0	0	1	1	0

can be put together to form what is known as a sociogram as in the following figure
(Fig. 1.2).

In the above figure, the circles represent the nodes, and the lines represent the
ties. Dark lines are strong connections, dash lines are weak connections, and regular
lines represent connections of medium strength. A tie with an arrow indicates a
directed tie. Here, *A* likes *B* (if this is a sociogram of liking), but *B* does not like *A*.
Ties with no direction are directionless, which could mean that they are reciprocated. For example, *E* likes *D* and *D* likes *E*. However, some reciprocated ties (such
as being brothers) do not lend themselves to having a direction.

Sociograms are a good way of looking at the picture of the social structure.
However, they are not easy to analyze, in particular for large networks. A better way
to do the analysis of the above network is by using matrices (a matrix is simply a
grid of numbers arranged in rows and columns) (Table 1.1).

The intersection of each row and column is called a cell. Each cell has a value
that can be either zero or one. If the actor in the row sends a tie to the actor in the
column, the cell value is one. Otherwise, it is zero. The main diagonal of the matrix
is the cells where the sending and receiving nodes are the same. Because we did not
allow nodes to be tied to themselves, the value of each of these cells is zero.
However, if we allow nodes to be tied to themselves, they can be drawn as arrows

Table 1.2 Matrix representation of the sociogram showing strengths of ties

	A	B	C	D	E
A	0	3	2	0	0
B	0	0	0	0	0
C	0	0	0	1	1
D	0	0	1	0	2
E	0	0	1	2	0

curving back to their nodes. In this case, the value of the main diagonal for any of these nodes is no more zero.

In addition to the simple representation of relationships between actors using zeros and ones to indicate the presence or absence of a tie between two nodes as done in the above table, we can also show the strength of the ties. For example, if the ties are multiplex, the values in the cells could be the number of different types of relationships between nodes. Simple metrics like "weak," "medium," or "strong" can also be used to indicate the strength of a relationship between pairs of nodes. They are translated as one, two, three, respectively. Nodes which have no tie between them are still coded zero (Table 1.2).

1.2.4   Homophily

An important requirement for the study of social networks is the identification of groups and the study of the relations between them. It is an important driver for maintaining stability in human and animal social communities over time, and it is a major criterion that governs the making of ties in social networks.

Homophily is the tendency of individuals to connect with others who share the same attitudes and beliefs. The tendency of individuals to associate with similar others based on gender, education, race, or other socioeconomic characteristics is very common in social communities. Coordination and cooperation are typically more successful between people who show some similarity to each other such that individuals in homophilic relationships are likely to hear about new ideas or ask for help from each other.

Homophily in the context of online social networking can be understood from the similarity of users who are using the network in terms of age, educational background, region, or profession. In the sense of corporate networks, homophily is translated as the similarity of professional or academic qualifications.

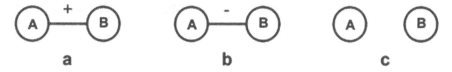

Fig. 1.3 Types of the relationships between two nodes

1.2.5 Dyads and Mutuality

A dyad is a pair of actors in a network potentially connected by a social relation. It is the simplest possible social group in which the transfer of information between the two nodes can be fast and easy. Dyads are among the concepts that characterize social networks. In the realm of corporations, dyadic links between organizations may allow the exchange of information and knowledge, joint venture, tangible and intangible resources, board interlocks, and many others. Each dyad can be in one of the three cases: a positive relationship, a negative relationship, and no relationship between the nodes of the dyad (empty dyad) (Fig. 1.3).

In Fig. 1.3a, b, nodes indicate individuals and each edge indicates either a positive or negative relationship. Figure c shows that node A and node B are not connected by any edge.

1.2.6 Balance and Triads

A triad is a network structure consisting of three actors and three dyads. Given a complete graph of three actors (triad), we can identify four different types of relationships, depending on the number of negative relationships between nodes: (a) a friend of my friend is my friend, (b) an enemy of my enemy is my friend, (c) a friend of my friend is my enemy, and (d) an enemy of my enemy is my enemy.

Once a sign is given to a link, the next question would be: how does that sign is going to interact with other signs in its local vicinity or with other signs at the network level?

Structural balance theory is the key concept in many applications of the signed graph theory. It tries to explain how a specific pattern of negative and positive signs can result in a different kind of relationships. The theory considers the possible ways in which triads can be signed: triads with an odd number of "+" edges are balanced, while triads with an even number of "-" edges are unbalanced. Imbalanced graph configurations usually create stress for individuals located on them.

Both the structural balance theory and signed graphs were developed to solve the subgrouping problem in social psychology. However, they found applications in other fields as well. They were found very helpful in predicting and explaining friendships and animosity changes in human communities, which is useful in the

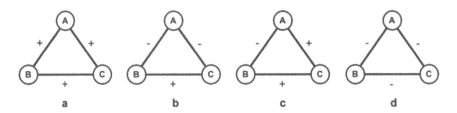

Fig. 1.4 Graph with three nodes in four states

analysis of enmity in tribal wars, political conflicts, or international relations. Let's consider a graph with four states as follows (Fig. 1.4).

The above graph is a type of signed graphs which have been studied since the 1950s. They are a special case of valued graphs in which ties are allowed to have one of two opposing values to convey the positive or negative sentiment. Examples of signed graphs include friend/foe, trust/distrust or like/dislike, esteem/disesteem, praise/blame, influence/negative influence, etc. They are very common in sociology and psychology but less common in fields such as physics and chemistry.

- In figure a, all the three actors have positive feelings, and there is no place for conflict among them. The configuration is coherent and lacks inner tensions between members.
- Figure b is also stable since two actors (B and C) share the same negative feeling towards actor A, but they like each other.
- Figure c is unstable because actors A and B have a negative feeling towards each other, while both have a positive feeling towards actor C which has to divide its loyalty between the other two actors.
- Figure d is also unstable and will eventually break down, as it has an odd number of negative signs.

In Fig. 1.4a, b, types of balanced subgraphs are shown, whereas in Fig. 1.4c, d, types of unbalanced graphs are presented. An obvious way to avoid unbalances in subgraphs is by sign shifting, which includes changing signs such that enmities (negative signs) become friendships (positive signs) or vice versa. Within real networks, stable configurations appear far more often than unstable configurations.

It should be noted here that a negative sign between two nodes does not mean the lack of tie between these two nodes. While a negative sign between two nodes is a clear mark of an inimical relationship, the absence of a tie between these nodes suggests the absence of interaction or communication between them.

1.2.7 Reciprocity

Reciprocity is a measure of the tendency towards building mutually directed connections between two actors. It refers to the number of reciprocated tie for a specific actor in a network. For example, if u connects to v, then v connects to u and vice versa. In real life scenarios, it is important to know whether received help is also given or whether given help is translated as help by the receiver.

For a given node v, reciprocity is the ratio between the number of nodes which have both incoming and outgoing connections from/to v, to the number of nodes which only have incoming connections from v. For an entire network, reciprocity is calculated as the fraction of edges that are reciprocated. Average reciprocity is calculated by averaging reciprocity values of all nodes in the network.

Reciprocity can be an indicator of the importance of a relationship between two actors. While a one-way relationship allows the transfer of information (e.g., messages) from only one side to another, a mutual relationship by this definition is stronger as it permits the transfer in both directions. In some cases, the relationship is skewed (i.e., information transfer in one direction is bigger than the other direction) toward one of the two actors, which can be an indication of differences in status and power between the two sides.

In friendship networks, such as Facebook.com, and since all friendship connections are expected to be mutual, reciprocity is 1 (or 100% if by percentage). However, this is not true for other online social networks (such as Twitter.com) where the "follow" model is the one that is used to represent relations.

1.3 Network Distribution

Measurements of network distribution are related to how nodes and edges are distributed in a network.

1.3.1 Distance Between Two Nodes

Distance is a network metric that allows the calculation of the number of edges between any pair of nodes in a network. Measuring distances between nodes in graphs is critical for many implementations like graph clustering and outlier detection. Sometimes, the distance measure is used to see if the two nodes are similar or not. Any commonly used shortest path calculation algorithm (e.g., Dijkstra) can be used to provide all shortest paths in a network with their lengths.

We can use the distance measure to calculate node eccentricity, which is the maximum distances from a given node to all other nodes in a network. It is also possible to calculate network diameter, which is the highest eccentricity of its nodes and thus represents the maximum distance between nodes.

In most social networks, the shortest path is computed based on the cost of transition from one node to another such that the longer the path value, the greater the cost.

Within a community, there might be many edges between nodes, but between communities, there are fewer edges.

1.3.2   Degree Centrality

In degree centrality metric, the importance of a node is determined by how many nodes it is connected to. It is a measurement of the number of direct links to other actors in the network. This means that the larger the number of adjacent nodes, the more important the node since it is independent of other actors that reach great parts of the network. It is a local measure since its value is computed based on the number of links an actor has to the other actors directly adjacent to it. Actors in social networks with a high degree of centrality serve as hubs and as major channels of information.

In social networks, for example, node degree distribution follows a power law distribution, which means that very few nodes have an extremely large number of connections. Naturally, those high-degree nodes have more impact in the network than other nodes and thus are considered more important. A node i's degree centrality $d(i)$ can be formulated as

$$d(i) = \sum_j m_{ij}$$

where $m_{ij} = 1$ if there is a link between nodes i and j and $m_{ij} = 0$ if there is no such link. For directed networks, it is important to differentiate between the in-degree centrality and the out-degree centrality.

Identifying individuals with the highest-degree centrality is essential in network analysis because having many ties means having multiple ways to fulfill the requirements of satisfying needs, becoming less dependent on other individuals, and having better access to network resources. Persons with the highest-degree centrality are often third parties and deal makers and able to benefit from this brokerage. For directed networks, in-degree is often used as a proxy for popularity (Fig. 1.5).

The above figure shows that node A and node B are at exceptional structural positions. All communications lines must go through them. This gives us a conclusion that both nodes, A and B, are powerful merely because of their excellent positions. However, such a finding is largely based on the nature of links and the nature of embedded relationships.

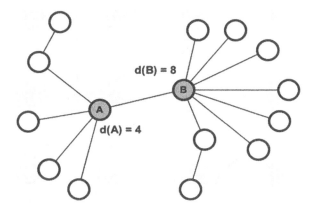

Fig. 1.5 Degree centrality of nodes

1.3.3 Closeness Centrality

Closeness centrality can be defined as how close, to a particular actor, other actors are. It is the sum of the geodesic distances of a node to all other nodes in the network. It computes the length of paths from one actor to other actors in the network.

That actor can be important if it is relatively close to the remaining set of actors in the network. The mathematical representation of closeness centrality, $C(i)$, is given as follows:

$$C(i) = \sum_j d_{ij}$$

where d_{ij} is the geodesic distance from node i to node j (number of links in the shortest path from node i to node j).

Closeness centrality is important to understand information dissemination in networks in the way that the distance between one particular node and others has an effect on how this node can receive from or send information (e.g., gossip) to other nodes. In social networks, this ability is limited by what is called "horizon of observability" which states that individuals have almost no sight into what is going on after two steps.

Because closeness centrality is based on the distance between network nodes, it can be considered the inverse of centrality because large values refer to lower centrality, whereas small values refer to high centrality. Computationally, the value of $C(i)$ is a number between 0 and 1, where higher numbers mean greater closeness (lower average distance) whereas lower numbers mean insignificant closeness (higher average distance) (Fig. 1.6).

In the above figure, the nodes in gray are the most central regarding closeness because they can reach the rest of nodes in the network easily and equally. They

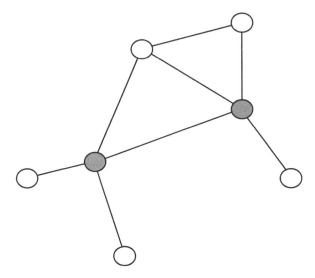

Fig. 1.6 Closeness centrality of nodes

have the ability to reach all other nodes in the fastest amount of time. The other nodes lack these privileged positions.

Because closeness centrality is based on shortest path calculations, its usefulness when applied to large networks can be brought into question in the way that closeness produces little variation in the results, which makes differentiating between nodes more difficult.

In information networks, closeness reveals how long it takes for a bit of information to flow from one node to others in the network. High-scoring nodes usually have shorter paths to the rest of nodes in the network.

1.3.4 Betweenness Centrality

Betweenness centrality can be described as how important an actor is, as a link between different networks. It represents the number of times an actor needs to pass via a given actor to reach another actor. Nodes with high betweenness centrality control the flow of information because they form critical bridges between other actors or groups of actors. Betweenness centrality of node i is calculated as follows:

$$b(i) = \sum_{j,k} \frac{g_{jik}}{g_{jk}}$$

where g_{jk} is the number of shortest paths from node (j) to node k (j and $k \neq i$) and g_{jik} is the number of shortest paths from node (j) to node k passing through the node (i).

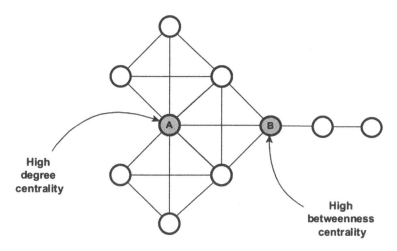

Fig. 1.7 Betweenness centrality of nodes

Betweenness centrality shows which nodes are likely pathways of information and can be used to determine how a graph will break apart of nodes are removed. Similarly, it is a way to identify those who act as bridges (also called boundary spanners) between two or more graph segments that otherwise would not be able to communicate to each other.

This measure touches on the importance that an actor can gain being in the middle of social communications of a network and to what extent in a society he/she is needed as a link in the chain of contacts.

The betweenness centrality of a node i is defined as the number of shortest paths between pairs of nodes that pass through node i. A vertex can have betweenness centrality value equals to 0 if it is not located at the shortest path between any two other vertices in the network, which points out a decrease in the social importance of the network (Fig. 1.7).

In the above illustration, node A has a good centrality value because it is located in the middle of a large part of the graph. Node B, on the other hand, has a good betweenness value because it connects two different sections of the network. It has gained more power because it presides over a communication bottleneck. All the communications between the nodes on the right segment of the graph and the left segment of it have to come through B. A person in that position would be a good nominee for any task related to directed advertising, information operations, or intelligent collection. Nevertheless, even though the bottleneck position can give power, it is still a source of a significant amount of stress.

In trust networks, the key concept is betweenness centrality. Because this measure describes that potential of the particular individual to control the communication among other individuals in a network, applying this concept to the school environment, for example, would help to find individuals whose friends are in different nonoverlapping social communities, and hence those individuals would be liaisons for all the intercommunity communications.

1.3.5   Eigenvector Centrality

Eigenvector centrality measurement describes the centrality of a person with regard to the global structure of the network. It assigns relative scores to all nodes in the network based on the concept that connections to nodes with high scoring contribute more to the score of the node in question than connections to nodes with low scoring.

It measures the extent to which a node is connected to well-connected nodes. It is computed by taking the principal eigenvector of the adjacency matrix. Calculating centrality in the way that eigenvector measure proposes differs from the way that degree measure applies to calculate centrality which is based on simply adding up the number of links of each node. Some people would be largely invisible in a network if we consider only network measures such as degree centrality, betweenness, or closeness. However, they would be so influential if it turns out that they are connected to some important people. While staying largely in the shadows, they can exploit the power given by knowing well-connected people to achieve their plans.

To calculate eigenvector centrality, we calculate the eigencomposition of the pairwise adjacency matrix of the graph, followed by choosing the eigenvector associated with the largest eigenvalue. Element i in the eigenvector gives the centrality of the i-th node (Fig. 1.8).

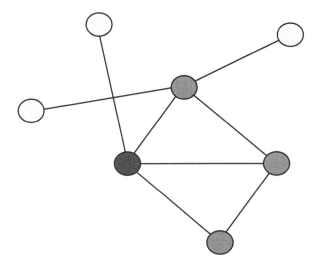

Fig. 1.8 Eigenvector centrality of nodes

1.3.6 PageRank

PageRank, which is a variant of the eigenvector centrality measure, calculates the importance of a Web page by considering the probability that a user visits this page based on the hyperlinks. It is one of the popular link-based ranking algorithms that ranks objects in a network according to the relative importance of each page within the object set which is determined by utilizing link information in the network. It has been successfully applied to the Web search problem. According to PageRank algorithm, the importance of a page is determined by the importance of the pages that it is linked to. A page is assigned a high rank if the sum of the ranks of its back-links is high. Otherwise, it is assigned a low rank.

For a directed network G with adjacency matrix A, the PageRank score of a page u is determined iteratively by the scores of its incoming neighbors:

$$PR(u) = \frac{1 - \alpha}{N} + \alpha \sum_{v} A_{vu} \ PR(v)/d_{out}(v)$$

where α is a damping factor that has a value between 0 and 1, N is the total number of nodes, and $d_{out}(v)$ is the degree of outgoing links of v.

In PageRank: nodes are Web pages, links are Web links, and state is the temporary "importance" of that node. It is calculated by forcedly assigning positive non-zero weights to all pairs of nodes to make the entire network strongly connected. Its coefficient matrix is a transition probability matrix that can be obtained by dividing each column of the adjacency matrix by the number of 1's in that column (Fig. 1.9).

Calculation: just one dominant eigenvector of the TPM of a strongly connected network always exists, with λ = 1. This shows the equilibrium distribution of the population over WWW. So, just solve x = Ax, and we will get the PageRank for all the Web pages on the World Wide Web.

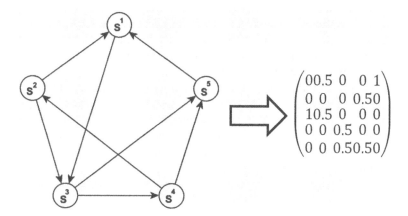

Fig. 1.9 PageRank conversion to a matrix

PageRank algorithm gives nontrivial results only for asymmetric networks. If links are symmetric (undirected), the PageRank values will be the same as node degrees.

In its basic form, PageRank is vulnerable to misuse by some people, and hence it needs to be regularly and secretly adjusted.

PageRank was proposed to index Web pages. However, it can also be applied to calculate centrality for directed graphs in social networks. Twitter can be a great example here!

1.3.7 Geodesic Distance and Shortest Path

For directed graphs, the geodesic distance d between two nodes (u, v) is defined as the number of edges between these two nodes, while the shortest path is defined as the path from u to v with minimum number of edges.

For undirected graphs, the distance d from u to v is the same distance as from v to u (i.e., $d(u, v) = d(v, u)$) because all paths can be reversed. Also, the distance from one node to itself is always zero (i.e., $d(u,u) = 0$), and the distance between two adjacent nodes (i.e., there exists only one edge between u and v) is one ($d(u,v) = 1$). If there is no path between u and v, then $d(u, v) = \infty$.

Many important network measurements are based on the concept of geodesic distance and shortest path. In real social networks, the distance between nodes can be small, while the number of edges can very high.

1.3.8 Eccentricity

Eccentricity is the maximum distances from a given node to all other nodes in a network. Different from whole-network measures (e.g., diameter and density) that give a value to an entire network, eccentricity is a popular path-based measure that gives value to each node in a network based on its direct and indirect connections. If we calculate the maximum eccentricity, which is the maximum distance between nodes, we get what is called "diameter." In addition to eccentricity, there are other popular path-based measures such as node clustering coefficient, closeness, and betweenness.

Formally, the eccentricity E of a node u (which is referred to as $E(u)$) is defined as the maximum distance between u and all other nodes in the network. This means that we need to compute the geodesic distance from u to all other nodes and choose the maximum value.

$$E(u) = \max_{v \in V} d(u, v)$$

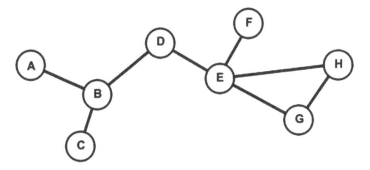

Fig. 1.10 Simple graph with eight nodes and eight edges

Calculating eccentricity is important for understanding how information can propagate from one node to other nodes. If information propagates from a given node towards some specific nodes in the graph in the smallest number of steps, it means that the given node has better propagation efficiency, although information does not always have to pass through the shortest paths of the network (Fig. 1.10).

The above figure is a graph with eight nodes and eight edges. We can see that the maximum eccentricity, which is network diameter, is 4. We can also see that node D has eccentricity 2, which means that the furthest nodes from D are located 2 hops away. Information propagated by node D can pass through nodes E and B in the smallest number of steps to reach the furthest nodes in the graph. However, node A, for example, has eccentricity 4 which means information needs to pass through at least three nodes (B, D, and E) and four edges to reach the furthest nodes.

1.3.9   Density

Density is defined as the degree to which network nodes are connected one to another. It can be used as a measure of how close a network is to complete. In the case of a complete graph (a graph in which all possible edges are present), density is equal to one. In real life, a dense group of objects has many connections among its entities (i.e., has a high density), while a sparse group has few of them (i.e., has a low density).

Formally, the density $D(G)$ of graph G is defined as the fraction of edges in G to the number of all possible edges. Density values range between zero and one [0, 1]. For undirected graphs, the possible number of edges is $n(n-1)/2$. Therefore,

$$D(G) = \frac{2m}{n(n-1)}$$

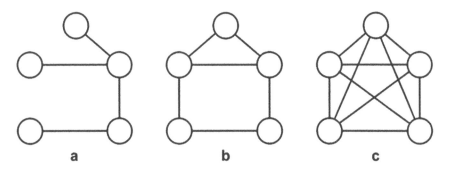

Fig. 1.11 Simple graph with five nodes and three states

where $m = |E|$ is the number of edges in G. If $D(G) = 1$, then the graph is complete and each pair of nodes is connected by an edge. However, if $D(G) = 0$, it means the graph has no edges at all and all nodes are isolated. Because any connected graph should have at least $n - 1$ edges, the minimum density for a connected graph is $2/n$.

If we are interested in calculating the density of ego-centric networks, we should consider the links around the focal node. The goal of such an analysis would be to explore the influence of the focal node on its neighbors in the subgroup that the node belongs. In case we want to calculate the density of socio-centric networks, we should consider the complete graph and the network constraints as well. Perfectly connected networks (every node is connected to all other nodes in the network) have a density of 1, while the possible number of edges for any graph is $n(n-1)/2$.

The following figure shows a graph with $n = 5$ nodes in three states, with an increasing number of edges in each state (Fig. 1.11).

The graph in Fig. 1.11a has $m = 4$ edges, resulting in a density $D(G) = (2*4)/(5*4) = 0.4$. In graph b, $m=6$, resulting in density $D(G) = (2*6)/(5*4) = 0.6$. Finally, in graph c, $m = 10$, resulting in density $D(G)=(2*10)/(5*4) = 1$, which means that the graph is fully connected.

In many online social networks (e.g., Facebook), the density is typically low. This is because each user is usually connected to tens or hundreds of other users, while the network itself has almost one billion users.

1.4 Network Segmentation

Measurements of network segmentation define network parts that are denser or more coherent than the other regions.

1.4.1 Cohesive Subgroups

Cohesive groups are communities in which the nodes (members) are connected to others in the same group more frequent than they are to those who are outside of the group, allowing all of the members of the group to reach each other. Within such a highly cohesive group, members tend to have strong homogenous beliefs. Connections between community members can be formed either through personal contacts (i.e., direct) or joint group membership (i.e., indirect). As such, the more tightly the individuals are tied into a community, the more they are affected by group standards.

Finding areas of a network in which nodes are more tightly connected to each other than those outside is referred to as "cohesive group analysis."

One of the examples of cohesive groups that is prevalent in graph theory (with roots in social network analysis) is called a "clique," which is a maximal complete subgraph. Another example is the "k-core" construct, which, in undirected networks, is defined as a subgraph having a minimum degree greater than or equal to k. K-cores are not necessarily cohesive groups, but they indicate areas of a graph which contain clique-like structures.

1.4.2 Cliques

A clique is a graph (or subgraph) in which every node is connected to every other node. Socially translated, a clique is a social grouping in which all individuals know each other (i.e., there is an edge between each pair of nodes). A triangle is an example of a clique of size three since it has three nodes and all the nodes are connected.

A maximal clique is a clique that is not a subset of any other clique in the graph. A clique with size greater than or equal to that of every other clique in the graph is called a maximum clique (Fig. 1.12).

In the above graph configurations, the maximum clique (the largest clique) is always of size 4. However, there are several maximal cliques of size three as well.

Finding maximum cliques in a network is an interesting and highly applicable problem in analyzing social relationships since it provides the largest set of common friendships. By comparing the sizes of the maximum friendship cliques over two social networks, we may get an idea about some aspects of group dynamics, such as teamwork, trust, and productivity.

Regarding friendship, which of your friends are also friends with one another? This question is asking about the ability to get the mutual friendships that exist within the social network (in this case, it is Facebook). The answer to this question is going to be through the detection of cliques, or mutual friendships, within an ego graph.

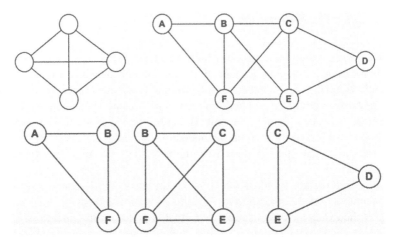

Fig. 1.12 Graph with different configurations

1.4.3 K-Cores

In undirected graphs, a k-core is a connected maximal induced subgraph having a minimum value greater than or equal to k. This means that each node has ties to at least k other nodes. These subgraphs are not necessarily cohesive groups, but they can tell about the areas which contain clique-like structures. K-cores can be used as a way to find cohesive subgroups in graphs.

K-core can be used by researchers as a sampling technique for collecting data from social networks, in particular, if the researcher is interested in extracting a group of participants from a larger diffuse group of participants. Members belonging to the k-core must have attended a well-defined activity during a specified time period, while those who do not belong to the k-core are light members.

1.4.4 Clustering Coefficient

Clustering coefficient is a measure of how much nodes tend to form dense subgraphs (also called cliques, communities, or clusters depending on their interpretation) in a network. For social networks, this can be interpreted as the probability that two friends of a single person are also themselves friends. As such, the clustering coefficient value is a number between zero and one. High values of clustering coefficient for a social network indicates that the network is showing a small-world phenomenon (in small-world networks, most nodes are homogeneous and can be reached by a small number of steps.)

Social networks were found to present a higher clustering coefficient than corresponding random networks, which means a higher tendency to create triangles. As

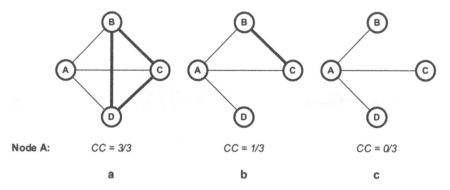

Node A: CC = 3/3   CC = 1/3   CC = 0/3

               a   b   c

Fig. 1.13 Clustering coefficient of a graph with four nodes

such, clustering coefficient can discriminate between social and random networks via highlighting nodes whose adjacent nodes are well connected to each other. Often, the measure is described as the measure of transitivity of a graph (transitivity is sometimes called whole-network clustering coefficient) (Fig. 1.13).

Figure a above shows a dense ego network (also known as clique) with a high clustering coefficient and much mutual trust. Figure b, on the other hand, has a single broadcast node and passive listeners. It has a low clustering coefficient.

The clustering coefficient C of a node i shows how its neighbors are connected with each other. Formally, it is the ratio between the total number of links connecting its neighbors and the total number of all possible links. The local (node) clustering coefficient is calculated as follows:

$$C_i = \binom{k_i}{2}^{-1} T(i) = \frac{2T(i)}{K_i\,(k_i - 1)}$$

where $T(i)$ is the number of distance triangles with node i and $K_i\,(k_i - 1)$ is the maximum number of possible connections in neighbors of i. A large C implies that the network is well connected locally to form a cluster.

Network average clustering is defined as:

$$C = \frac{1}{n} \sum_{i \in v} C_i$$

The computation of the node clustering coefficient C_i can be done in time $O(n^2)$ in the worst case via counting all edges connected directly to node i. The network clustering coefficient can be computed by counting all closed triplets. A brute-force approach can be used to examine network clustering coefficient by examining the combination of nodes, with time complexity equals $O(n^3)$. Another approach proposes the use of fast matrix multiplication on the adjacency matrix representation of graph G to solve triplet finding, counting, and node counting in $O(n^{2.376})$ time and

$O\left(n^{2}\right)$ space. In bipartite graphs, where triangles do not exist, clustering coefficient is trivially equal to zero.

1.4.5 Core/Periphery

The concept of core and periphery states that in any directed graph, nodes should belong to one of two classes: (1) the core, in which nodes are embedded in a coherent subgraph, and (2) the periphery, in which nodes are loosely connected. The nodes of the core are much more connected to each other than with the periphery.

We can also define core and periphery at a smaller size if we consider the k-core structure. Nodes that are part of the k-core structure are the core nodes, while nodes that stay outside it are the light nodes (or periphery nodes).

Networks in general exhibit structural changes over time, denoting the addition or deletion of nodes and/or edges. For example, social relations appear and disappear according to certain social events happening in the society. Several factors can have an influence on how this change can go such as the individual properties and behavior of actors and similarity characteristics of pairs of nodes. The study of dynamic behavior of networks that evolve over time is called dynamic network analysis (DNA), and it differs from traditional social network analysis, which proposes that the network is static during analysis. While DNA is more concerned with the activity of network actors and their interactions, SNA concentrates on the structural properties of a network.

On evolving networks also, nodes may not stay in one case all the time as they may move from one network class to the other. Nodes at the core, for example, can be either long-term core nodes (staying there for a long time) or hort-term core nodes (after staying at the core for a short time, they either move to the periphery or are eliminated) depending on the behavior that nodes show in the network and also on the behavior of the network as a whole.

In the blogosphere domain, core and periphery notations can be understood such that core blogs are the blogs that are more read, more cited in media, and more linked to other blogs, but with poor connections to other blogs in the domain. On online social networks, a person with many connections (i.e., friends) stay at the core of the local social network and benefit from the advantages that are offered by this unique position. Compared to other persons who are located at the periphery, they are in a good social health.

1.4.6 Blockmodels

Blockmodeling is an analytic method that uses data partitioning in a social network to classify actors based on their patterns of ties to others. It is one of the earliest methods for detecting social groups (communities) and was considered a revolutionary method in the documentation of relationship patterns and the identification of social positions.

The general idea of blockmodels is that nodes are partitioned (based on some equivalence measure) into discrete subgroup positions. These positions are then checked, for each pair of positions, for the presence or absence of relational ties. Several equivalence measures are used for this purpose such as the structural equivalence, the regular equivalence, and the stochastic equivalence.

The first study that used blockmodels to discover communities in social networks was conducted in 1941. Symmetric data on the social activities of 18 women was collected over a period of 9 months during which the various subsets of these women had met in a series of 14 social events.

Because blockmodeling has the benefit of identifying individuals who can play the same role in the same or a different population, it was used to identify role structures among business managers using social ties. It was also used to understand the structure of co-citation networks and the structure of personality types in small groups.

1.4.7 Hierarchical Clustering

Hierarchical clustering is one of earliest methods for clustering data using a similarity matrix. It is part of a wider classification criterion for clustering algorithms: hierarchical (e.g., hierarchical clustering) vs. non-hierarchical (e.g., k-means). Members of the first kind build a full hierarchy of clusters, while members of the other kind provide a fixed number of data clusters. On social networks, hierarchical clustering means that we partition network nodes (actors) into groups of similar nodes using some distance measure.

Two implementations were developed for the hierarchical clustering algorithm: agglomerative and divisive. The agglomerative version starts with clustering all data items into clusters (or groups) based on a distance metric. The closest pair of clusters is then merged by moving up the hierarchy into a single cluster, while the correlation between data items of different clusters decreases as we move from the bottom (leaves) to the top (root). This step is repeated until all items are clustered into one single cluster.

This algorithm is commonly used by the social community for community detection. Using this approach, we can define a measure of similarity x_{ij} between a pair of nodes (i,j) based on the given network structure. We start with the pair having the highest similarity score (i.e., minimum distance) and then add more pairs which will decrease similarity. The number of desired number of clusters (groups) of users is left to the analyst.

The choice of the number of clusters can be made in different ways such as by calculating the classification error as a function of the number of clusters and finding the knee of the resulting curve.

Finding out which clusters to merge can also be done in different ways. For example, the complete-linkage method considers the distance between two clusters to be equal to the greatest distance from any data item in one cluster to any data item in the other cluster. The single-linkage method considers the distance between any two clusters to be equal to the shortest distance from and a data item in the first cluster and any data item in the other cluster. The average-linkage clustering method considers the distance between one cluster and another to be equal to the average distance from any data item in the first cluster to any data item in the other cluster. Although the single-linkage clustering method suffers from what is called "chain effect" and is less suited to detect spherical clusters, it is still more commonly used since it has the ability to detect elongated and irregular clusters. The complete-linkage clustering method is not used in general because it is highly sensitive to outliers.

The divisive version of this algorithm does the reverse such that it starts with one single cluster and subdivides it into smaller pieces. The agglomerative version is more commonly used than the divisive one.

1.5   Recent Developments in Network Analysis

There are many topics on network analysis that recently drew huge interest from researchers due to their importance for many applications. We discuss here four of them: community detection, link prediction, protein-protein interaction networks, and recommendation systems.

1.5.1   Community Detection

The task of community detection (or graph clustering) is to discover subsets of nodes (clusters) of connected communities in which nodes have many internal edges and few external edges. Identifying communities in graphs is feasible only if the graph is sparse, which means that number of links $m \approx$ number of nodes n. Community detection has many applications such as modeling large-scale online networks and understanding the social structure of organizations.

Many networks exhibit a collection of distinct groups (or communities) such that there are very few edges between communities and many edges between nodes inside a community. A community is described as having a higher connectivity within the community and lower connectivity to the remaining part of the network.

Detecting communities in a graph is NP-complete. The problem of community detection is somehow similar to "clustering" in computer science. Extracting all communities from a given network is not a straightforward task especially in the case of large or complex networks because it necessitates the exploration of the entire graph.

Formally, the problem of community detection can be given as follows: given graph $G = (V; E)$, a community C can be defined as a subgraph of G comprising a set $V_c \in V$ of objects that share some similarity.

Community detection has been an active research area in different fields such as computer science, social science, biology, and psychology. In the study of social networks, the discovery of communities plays an important role as it helps to find segments of the population which are well connected. In sociology, the aim of community detection is to find social groupings based on networks of social interactions.

Many algorithms have been proposed for this purpose. They can be divided into three categories: divisive, agglomerative, and optimization algorithms. K-cliques, modularity optimization, and link communities are some of the popular methods in the stream of community detection, in addition to hundreds of other algorithms that take roots from information systems, computer science, and Bayesian inference.

In the realm of computer science, community identification is closely related to graph partitioning, in which the aim is to find partitions in the graph which minimize the number of inter-partition edges. In sociology, scientists have developed various methods for extracting communities which are based on the notion of cohesive subgroups. Hierarchical clustering and clique-like structures lend themselves well to the definition of cohesive subgroups and are commonly used by the social science for community detection.

The identification of communities in networks does not mean that communities should be disjoint partitions of nodes in the network. Rather, communities are expected to allow the sharing of members, which is called "overlapping communities." It should be noted here that the identification of communities can be done for static as well as for dynamic communities (also known as temporal community detection) in which communities evolve as the individuals themselves.

The most popular algorithm for identifying communities in networks was proposed by Girvan and Newman who identified three types of betweenness measures: geodesic edge betweenness, random-walk edge betweenness, and current-flow edge betweenness. The study marked the beginning surge of interest in community detection within network science. They found that there is no need to define the number of groups in advance or put restrictions on their size. Rather, these groups can be detected via natural divisions among the nodes. They applied a divisive approach in which edges are progressively removed from the network followed by removing links that lie between communities since they are considered bottlenecks. The work was followed by hundreds of works drawing from different disciplines.

In computer science, the problem is tackled by decomposing a network into a predefined number of groups of nodes. These groups almost have the same size, and the number of edges between two groups is minimized. First, the network is divided into two groups. A number of subsequent divisions are conducted next until the required number of groups is reached.

Future directions of community detection should consider issues such as how to handle large-size data, dynamic networks, the computational complexity of networks, unknown numbers and sizes of communities in advance, and how to manage nodes that belong to more than one community (also called overlapping communities).

1.5.2 Link Prediction

Link prediction is about inferring the links between nodes based on their attributes and the global patterns of links in the social network. This is important in situations where the links in the network may not be known in advance. Although the early approaches to link prediction were developed for dealing with undirected and unweighted graphs, recent work in this area also tried manage issues related to directed, weighted, and evolving networks.

Leveraging the idea that links in a network do not form randomly, we can infer that two nodes that share some similarity (e.g., similarity in their geo-location information or their pattern of connections with other nodes) are more likely to be connected to one another.

The link prediction problem can be formally given as follows: given a network graph $G = (V, E)$, the task here is to predict whether there will be a link between two nodes u and v, where both u and $v \in V$ and $e(u, v) \notin E$.

Finding node similarities can be done using measures for analyzing the proximity of nodes in a network such as a degree distribution, common neighbors, preferential attachment, Jaccard coefficient, Leicht-Holme-Newman Index, and Kart Index.

In addition to node-based methods as an easy method for link prediction, other techniques were also developed for this purpose. For example, likelihood-based methods make an assumption about the network organization and structure and use that assumption to predict missing links. Other techniques for link prediction include matrix factorization and feature-based classification, where the latter method tries to select a number of features from the network topological or non-topological set of features such that the chosen features should effectively describe the link likelihood appropriately. In general, methods that use features to train a binary classification model consider the link prediction problem as a supervised classification task, while methods that are based on node similarity look at link prediction as an unsupervised task.

The task of link prediction can be classified into three categories: (1) predict missing or unobserved links in a network, (2) predict the links that are likely to be formed in the near future, and (3) predict whether there will be an interaction between a pair of nodes with a previously observed association. This task, however, can become more complicated if the attributes or identities of nodes are not completely available.

Link prediction has several applications in areas like network evolution as it allows the study of the mechanisms that control the formation and deletion of nodes in these networks. Link prediction is also used by e-commerce systems for building product recommendations. In the healthcare sector, link prediction can be used to identify the interactions between drugs and proteins or between diseases and proteins.

In social networks, link prediction uses similarity of users to predict or recommend new friendships. For example, a high similarity between two users increases the probability that these would create a friendship in the future. As such, the problem of link prediction can be generalized to another issue (homophily) which states that people tend to friend others who carry similar personal attributes such as gender, race, age, education, or religion. It is also possible to predict whether there will be an interaction between two people upon their first face-to-face meeting, or predicting the risk of disclosure of critical information under certain circumstances by some individual.

It is also useful in predicting new alliances between nations. In coauthorship networks, link prediction can be used to measure the likelihood of coauthorship for two authors.

1.5.3 Spatial Networks

A spatial network is a graph in which nodes are embedded in a metric space, which means that the nodes are located in a space equipped with a particular metric. Spatial data have a spatial reference, i.e., coordinate values and a special system of reference for these coordinates.

The study of spatial networks is of crucial importance in many areas ranging from urbanism to epidemiology. The Internet is an obvious example of spatial networks as it consists of a set of nodes (i.e., routers) linked by edges (i.e., cables) with different lengths and latency times. Drawing a map with various types of communication networks (e.g., cars and trains) is another example of spatial networks.

In urban spatial networks (transportation networks), edges represent street segments, while nodes are the junctions where two or more edges (streets) intersect. However, such networks can at times be represented as tripartite networks rather than bipartite networks. As such, three elements are associated with the representation of such networks: edges, paths along which passengers can navigate; nodes, the intersections where two more edges interest; and buildings, the locations where traffic from streets goes indoor areas or vice versa.

If we want to build a spatial network, we need first to draw a graph (i.e., nodes and edges) of a system and then add the physical representations to the network, which will help better understand the importance of physical distances between elements to the operation of networks.

1.5.4 Protein-Protein Interaction Networks

Protein-protein interaction networks are a type of biological networks. Nodes in these networks represent individual proteins, and the interactions between proteins (PPI) are the edges. Such interactions take the form of two or more proteins binding together to carry out a specific biological function. Analyzing PPI networks is essential for a full understanding of the molecular basis for most of the diseases.

There are several ways to study interactions between proteins among which the "yeast two-hybrid system" is the method commonly used to discover protein-protein interactions and protein-DNA interactions. The way it works is that it tests for physical interactions between a pair of proteins or a single protein and a DNA molecule.

Because the interactions between proteins are crucial, they have become the most intensely analyzed networks in biology. These networks are formed by biomedical events or electrical forces (or both). They have been studied in different areas such as biochemistry, molecular dynamics, signal transduction, and others. Other types of biological networks include gene co-expression, metabolic, signaling, neuronal, between-species interaction, and within-species interaction networks, as well food webs.

Connectedness in protein-protein interaction networks is critical for survival such that proteins with a high degree of connectedness are more crucial for survival than proteins with lesser degrees.

1.5.5 Recommendation Systems

Recommendation systems (or recommenders) are software tools that give suggestions for items that are very likely to be of interest to a particular user. They have the benefit of increasing the number of items sold, selling more diverse items, increasing the user satisfaction, increasing user fidelity, and providing a better understanding of what the user wants.

They became extremely common in recent years due to the popularity of online retailers in a variety of areas such as books, music, CDs, movies, clothes, news, research articles, etc. Famous online services that show recommendations to visitors include Amazon.com and eBay.com and several online music recommendation engines such as Lastfm.com, and Pandora.com create playlists based on user selection and attributes of songs such as genre, musician, and artist.

Providing recommendations to users can be done in one of two ways: content-based filtering or collaborative filtering. In the content-based filtering (CBF) approaches, the user will be recommended items similar to the ones he/she preferred in the past. Collaborative filtering (CF) approaches consider a user's past behavior (e.g., items previously purchased or rated) and a similar decision made by other users to predict items that the user may have an interest in. They are based on

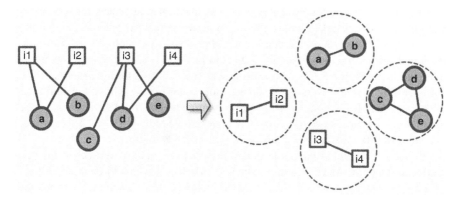

Fig. 1.14 Converting a two-mode network into subnetworks

the premise that similar users like similar items. A user-item network can be built according to what every user has bought/liked in the past. The relationship between two users becomes stronger if they have more things in common. This network is a type of what is called two-mode network since it has two types of nodes, users, and items. A simple analysis process to divide that network into two subnetworks can be applied next to put the items that are similar in one group. Recommendations are given next based on how strong that relationship is. Such type of recommendation systems are also referred to as social recommendation systems, which also have roots in the theory of homophily (Fig. 1.14).

The above figure shows how it is possible to extract several user-user and item-item subnetworks from the main user-item network in which users are linked to the items they bought or liked.

Apart from recommendations in online businesses, some social networking websites (like Facebook.com) give recommendations to registered users to help them make new friends and expand their networks, based on existing social connections and their similar interests. The goal here is to predict new acquaintances with people who were not previously connected. Such networks are sometimes called Friend Recommender Systems (FRSs). This problem in this sense can also be considered a link prediction problem.

1.6 iGraph

There are various tools for social network analysis such as MuxViz, NetworkX (used throughout this study), and iGraph, in addition to a number of standard methods to visualize data such as box plots, scatter plots, word clouds, and decision trees. Because iGraph is a very powerful data visualization package, we are going to use it in this section for building graphs through RStudio (a development environment for R software).

iGraph is a software for the analysis and visualization of large networks. It allows analysts to perform tasks that are related to network analysis such as community discovery, cohesive groups, structural holes, dyad, triad, and motif count. It also has implementations for more specific graph problems, such as minimum spanning trees and network flows. It is an open source software (OSS) that can run on different operating systems such as Windows, Linux, and OS X. iGraph currently has interfaces for C, R, Python, and Ruby programming languages. We will consider the use of iGraph within R programming language and RStudio interface. This requires that we install R software first followed by installing RStudio.

We use the layout() function to determine the placement of vertices in the network and the plot() function to draw the network. It is possible through RStudio to explore the various functionalities included in any of these functions by executing ?<function name> function.

We need to install the iGraph package from packages → install → iGraph. After we install iGraph, we need to load the package iGraph into RStudio.

```
require(igraph)
```

Let's build simple graphs to see how the package works. We use a vector (c) in which the first element points to the second, the third points to the fourth, and so on. We use spaces to separate between pairs of nodes. We also determine the number of nodes (optional).

```
g <- graph(c(1,2, 1,3, 2,3, 3,4, 4,5, 4,6, 6,7, 6,8), n=9)
```

To show how the edges of the graph are connected, execute the following command:

```
print(g)
```

The result will be

```
IGRAPH D--- 9 8 --
+ edges:
[1] 1->2 1->3 2->3 3->4 4->5 4->6 6->7 6->8
```

To plot the graph use the plot() function. We will also define the color of the nodes (Fig. 1.15).

```
plot(g, vertex.color="yellow")
```

The result will be a disconnected graph that has two partitions: the largest one contains eight vertices, while the other component has only one vertex (isolate).

It is also possible to draw random graphs using iGraph. We will draw a tree with 30 vertices and three children for each vertex (Fig. 1.16).

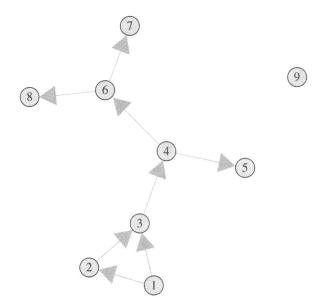

Fig. 1.15 Simple graph representation in iGraph

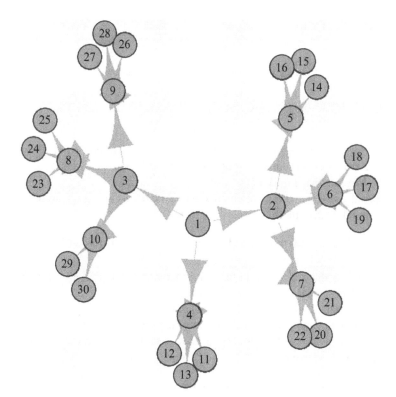

Fig. 1.16 Random graph representation in iGraph

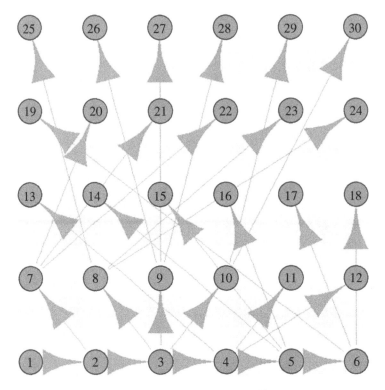

Fig. 1.17 Random graph representation with the davidson.harel layout

```
g <- graph.tree(30, 3)
plot(g)
```

There are different layouts to plot this very same graph. For example, we have the circle, fruchterman.reingold, graphopt, kamada.kawai, gem, etc. Let's try the davidson.harel layout (Fig. 1.17).

We can also use the tkplot() function to move the points of a graph around, which gives us an interactive plotting pane.

```
tkplot(g, layout=layout.kamada.kawai, vertex.color="yellow")
```

The result of the above execution is an interactive pane that allows us to drag nodes and change their positions, which is a great feature.

There is another function called rglplot() that allows to fly through the graph in a pseudo 3D manner and get a deeper insight of the graph structure.

Before we can use this function, we need to install the rgl package. On RStudio, choose packages → install → rgl.

```
rglplot(g, layout=layout.kamada.kawai, vertex.color="cyan")
```

Chapter 2
Network Basics

This chapter introduces the concept of a network, which is obviously the core object of network analysis. We will discuss topics such as types of networks, network measures, installation and use of NetworkX library, network data representation, basic matrix operations, and data visualization.

2.1 What Is a Network?

A network can be a specialized type of mathematical graph or interconnected systems. Hence, it is not far from a graph, which implies the visual representation of a set of nodes and edges. Network nodes may represent web pages, people, organizations, articles, places, and many other things.

2.2 Types of Networks

Networks in real world fall into one of the following four major types:

- *Information networks*: Man-made networks in which data items are linked together in some way. The best-known example is the World Wide Web (WWW), a network in which the vertices represent Web pages consisting of text, pictures, and other information. Navigation from one page to another is done with the use of hyperlinks that represent edges. Other examples of information networks—even though having social aspects to them—include email communications, social-networking websites such as Facebook and Twitter, weblogs, and citation.
- *Technological networks*: Man-made networks that are designed to distribute commodity or resources. Technological networks grew up mostly during the last

© Springer International Publishing AG 2017   33
M.Z. Al-Taie, S. Kadry, *Python for Graph and Network Analysis*, Advanced
Information and Knowledge Processing, DOI 10.1007/978-3-319-53004-8_2

century making use of the emerging advancements in technology. One of the greatest examples is the Internet, a global technological network that consists of communication devices to link computers and other information equipment together (Fig. 2). Other examples include power grids, transportation networks, delivery and distribution networks, and telephone networks.

- *Biological networks*: Networks that represent patterns of interaction between biological elements. Examples of biological networks include (1) biochemical networks: networks that represent patterns of interaction and mechanisms of control at the molecular level in biological cells. (2) Neural networks: networks that connect neurons in the human brain and the central nervous systems of animals. (3) Ecological networks: networks of ecological interactions between species.
- *Social networks*: Networks in which vertices represent people and edges represent some form of social interaction between vertices including friendship, kinship, information flow, disease outbreak, etc.
- *Complex networks:* Wikipedia defines complex networks as networks with nontrivial topological features—features that do not occur in simple networks such as lattices or random graphs but often happen in real graphs. Examples of complex networks include biological networks (e.g., proteins, molecules, and chemical reactions), brain networks (e.g., physiological networks and neurological pathways), social networks, and the Internet. Complex networks typically have new emergent properties that are held by the individual units. Social networks are kind of complex networks because they show nontrivial topological features that do not occur in simple networks. Typically, a network is a set of nodes interconnected via links. Nodes and links can be anything depending on the context. For example, in the Internet, nodes refer to routers and links refer to optical fibers. In WWW, nodes represent document files and links represent hyperlinks. In the scientific citation network, nodes represent papers and links represent citations. In a social network, node individuals and links represent relations. Example generators of complex networks include Erdos-Renyi graph, Watts-Strogatz graph, Barabasi-Albert graph, and Random-lobster graph.

2.3 Properties of Networks

Networks are characterized by two types of properties: static and dynamic.

1. Network static properties are fixed. They are the properties of nodes and edges and do not change over time once the network is established (e.g., density, shortest paths, and centralities).
2. Network dynamic properties are not fixed. They can be processes running on the underlying network substrate (e.g., population dynamics on ecological networks and disease infection on social networks). They can also be the dynamical processes of complex networks and their structural/statistical properties such as

social network formation, food web formation over ecological/evolutionary time scales, the growth of the Internet and WWW, the growth of scientific citation networks, and the effects of node/link removal or rewiring.

Despite having some differences, all types of networks share the following common characteristics:

- *Transitivity (clustering)*, which means that if node A is connected to node B and node B is connected to node C, then there is a high probability that node A is also connected to node C.
- *Network robustness and vulnerability*, which means that networks are susceptible to dynamic topological changes caused by external forces (e.g., node removal). Node removal can be the result of the (1) error, which is a random removal of nodes, and (2) attack, which is a selective removal of most connected nodes. Node removal leads to changes in characteristic path length and connectivity. If node removal goes on further, the network will eventually fall apart (fragmentation). However, not all networks show the same behavior in response to node removal.
- *Mixing patterns*, which refers to the tendency of vertices to be connected to other vertices that are like (or unlike) them in some way. Social networks tend to show an assortative mixing pattern. For example, people of a similar age are more likely to be friends and people of the same race tend to associate together. On the other hand, technological and biological networks tend to show a disassortative mixing pattern.
- *Community structure*, which means that networks may have high edge density between nodes of the same group while having low edge density between nodes from different groups.

Additionally, scientists found additional properties which are more relevant to large networks (i.e., networks with thousands, hundreds of thousands, or even millions of vertices):

- The tendency to establish groups of acquaintances and friends to form cliques (maximum connected components) where everyone knows everyone else.
- Node degree tends to show a power law distribution, which is the probability that a random node has a certain number of edges.

2.4   Network Measures

We provide a brief definition to the measures that are widely used in network analysis research. Most of these measures have been imported from graph theory:

1. *Aggregate constraint*: the sum of the dyadic constraint on all the ties of a particular vertex.

2. *Average degree*: A measure of the structural cohesion of a network. To calculate the average degree, all degrees are summed up first and then divided by the total number of nodes in the network.
3. *Degree distribution*: frequency of the degrees of nodes. Graphs with power law degree distribution are called scale-free. It gives a rough profile of how the connectivity is distributed within the network.
4. *Average shortest path*. Average shortest path length over all pairs of nodes characterizes how large the world represented by the network is, where a small length implies that the network is well connected globally.
5. *Eccentricity*: max shortest path length from each node.
6. *Diameter*: the longest shortest-path distance over all pairs of nodes in the network (or max eccentricity in the network). The goal of measuring diameter measure is to index the extensiveness of the network, which means how far apart the two furthest nodes in the network are from each other. Radius is the min eccentricity in the network.
7. *Dyad*: A dyad is a pair of nodes connected via one or more ties.
8. *Dyadic constraint*: The dyadic constraint on vertex u projected by the tie between vertex u and vertex v is the extent to which u has more and stronger ties with neighbors that are strongly connected with vertex v.
9. *Geodesic*. A geodesic is the shortest path between two vertices.
10. *Average geodesic distance*: the mean of the shortest path lengths among all connected pairs in the ego network.
11. *Multiplicity*: the number of times a particular (ordered or unordered pair of vertices) line occurs in a network.
12. *Popularity*: The popularity of a vertex in a directed network is the number of arcs that it receives.
13. *Triad*: a subnetwork consisting of three nodes.

The type of analyses applied to graphs (such as cardinality, network traversals, and community detection) has many mathematical underpinnings. Therefore, and for this purpose, we will use one of the greatest Python libraries for network analysis which is NetworkX.

2.5   NetworkX

NetworkX is a Python language software package and an open-source tool for the creation, manipulation, and study of the structure, dynamics, and functions of complex networks. It is a computational network modeling tool and not a software tool development. It can load, store, and analyze networks, generate new networks, build network models, and draw networks. The first public release of the library, which is all based on Python, was in April 2005, and the library can engage with languages other than Python such as C, C++, and FORTRAN.

NetworkX, the Python-based graph toolkit, is a type of memory graph databases. The amount of work that we can do is directly proportional to the amount of working memory on the machine that we are running our system. Improving the performance can be done through reducing the size of data or considering the use of a machine with larger memory.

Although NetworkX is not ideal for large-scale problems with fast processing requirements, it is a great option for real-world network analysis:

- Most of the core algorithms rely on extremely fast legacy code.
- It uses standard graph algorithms.
- It has an extensive set of native readable and writable formats.
- It is easy to install and use on the main platforms with a strong online up-to-date documentation.
- It is ideal for representing networks of different types like classic graphs, random graphs, and synthetic networks.
- It takes advantage of Python's ability to import data from outside sources.
- NetworkX includes many graph generator functions and facilities to read and write graphs in many formats such as .edgelist, .adjlist, .gml, .graphml, .pajek, etc.

However, some other packages and tools are also available in Python for network analysis and visualization including:

- PyCX Project: http://pycx.sf.net/
- ComplexNetworkSim
- SimPy
- graph-tool [http://graph-tool.skewed.de/]
- pyGraphViz (GraphViz) [http://www.graphviz.org/]
- igraph [http://igraph.org/]
- python-graph
- gephi [http://gephi.org/]

2.6 Installation

- I developed this book using Anaconda from Continuum Analytics, which is a free Python distribution that includes all the packages you'll need to run the code (and lots more).
- I found Anaconda easy to install. By default it does a user-level installation, not system level, so you do not need administrative privileges. Moreover, it supports both Python 2 and Python 3. You can download Anaconda from Continuum.
- If you do not want to use Anaconda, you will need the following packages:
  - *NetworkX* for network analysis
  - *Numpy* for basic numerical computation
  - *SciPy* for scientific computation including statistics
  - *Matplotlib* for visualization

- Although these are commonly used packages, they are not included with all Python installations, and they can be hard to install in some environments. If you have trouble installing them, I strongly recommend using Anaconda or one of the other Python distributions that include these packages.

To print the list of graph types available from NetworkX package, simply issue the following command:

```
In:   print[s for s in dir(nx) if s.endswith('graph')]
Out:
      ['LCF_graph', 'barabasi_albert_graph', 'barbell_graph',
      'binomial_graph', 'bull_graph', 'caveman_graph',
      'chordal_cycle_graph', 'chvatal_graph',
      'circulant_graph', 'circular_ladder_graph',
      'complete_bipartite_graph', 'complete_graph',
      'complete_multipartite_graph', 'connected_caveman_graph',
      ..........]
```

In IPython, we can type class object? to get details about this object. Let's get some information about the ladder graph object:

```
In:   nx.ladder_graph?
Out:
      Signature:
      nx.ladder_graph(n, create_using=None)

      Docstring:
      Return the Ladder graph of length n.

      This is two rows of n nodes, with each pair connected by a single
      edge.

      Node labels are the integers 0 to 2*n - 1.
      File:
      c:\users\zuhair\anaconda2\lib\site-
      packages\networkx\generators\classic.py
      Type:
      function
```

Let's take two examples to see how NetworkX can be used, which will help develop our understanding and intuition of graphs.

Example 1:
In this example, we will import NetworkX library under the name nx. With the help of this library, we can, for instance, create an undirected graph by initiating an instance of the class nx.Graph().

We will first create a simple directed graph using nx.Graph(), and then add one node using nx.add_node() method, and add a set of nodes using nx.add_nodes_ from() method which returns a list of item:

```
In [1]: import networkx as nx
        %matplotlib inline
        import matplotlib.pyplot as plt
In:   g = nx.Graph()
      g.add_node(1)

In:   g.nodes()
Out:  [1]

In:   g.add_nodes_from([2, 3, 4])
      g.nodes()
Out:  [1, 2, 3, 4]
```

Now, these nodes need be connected which will be done using nx.add_edge() method. To add a list of edges, rather than one single edge each time, we can use nx.add_edges_from() method and pass to it a list of tuples of nodes to connect to.

```
In [7]: g. add_edge(1, 2)
In [8]: g.edges()
Out [8]: [(1, 2)]
In [9]: g.add_edges_from([(3, 4), (5, 6)])
In [10]: g.edges()
In [10]: [(1, 2), (3, 4), (5, 6)]
```

The ad_weighted_edges_from() method is used to add edges that have weights associated with them. Weights, in this case, can represent distance, frequency, type of relationship, or others. In this method, we pass the two nodes that we want them to get connected as well as the connection weight. Optionally, data = Ture argument can be used when we call the edges method if we want the edge data to be displayed alongside the resulting list. Note that adding edges between nodes that do not yet exist does not give an error but rather make these nodes get automatically created.

```
In [11]: g.add_weighted_edges_from([(7, 8, 1.5), (9, 10,
         3.5)])
In [12]: g.edges(data = True)
Out [12]: [(1, 2, {}),
           (3, 4, {}),
           (5, 6, {}),
           (7, 8, {'weight': 1.5}),
           (9, 10, {'weight': 3.5})]
```

To add edges using unpack edge tuples, we can issue the following command:

```
In [13]: e = (2, 7)
In [14]: g.add_edge(*e)
```

We can also change the color and size of nodes. To visualize the resulting network, we need to issue the following command:

Fig. 2.1 Simple
undirected graph in
NetworkX

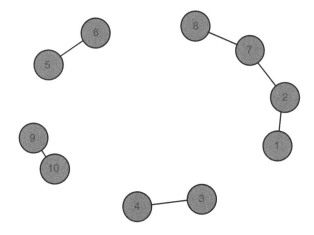

In [15]: nx.draw_networkx(g, node_color='green', node_size=700) (Fig. 2.1)

2.7   Matrices

A matrix is an alternative way to represent and summarize network data. It is an array of elements that contains the same information as a graph. Matrix operations have been widely used for definition and calculation in SNA.

Both graph and matrix operations have served as the foundations of many concepts in the analysis of social networks. However, matrices are more suitable for computation and computer analysis.

In general, a matrix is a collection of rows and columns. Column-row intersection cells show how the elements in rows look at the items in columns. Matrices have the following common types:

- *Column matrix*: a matrix with vertical entries only.
- *Row matrix*: a matrix with horizontal entries only.
- *Square matrix*: a matrix in which the number of rows is equal to the number of columns.
- *Identity matrix*: a square matrix in which the values of the main diagonal are set to 1s, while the values of all other elements are set to 0s.
- *Diagonal matrix*: a square matrix in which the values of all elements (except the main diagonal) are set to 0s, while the values of the main diagonal are not necessarily set to 1s.
- *Symmetric matrix*: a square matrix that is equal to its transpose.
- *Skew-symmetric matrix*: a square matrix where its negative is equal to its transpose.
- *Triangle matrix*: a square matrix in which all coefficients below the main diagonal are 0s.
- *Null matrix*: a matrix where all elements are zero.

2.8   Types of Matrices in Social Networks

Three types of matrices are used to represent data in social networks. These are:

2.8.1   Adjacency Matrix

The adjacency matrix is a matrix with rows and columns at plot by nodes, where element A_{ij} shows the number of links going from node i to node j (becomes symmetric for undirected graph). For directed graphs, the adjacency matrix takes the following form:

	A	B	C	D	E
A	0	1	0	0	0
B	1	0	0	1	0
C	0	0	0	1	1
D	1	0	1	0	0
E	1	0	1	0	0

Value (1) denotes the presence of relation (edge) between node A and node B while value (0) means no such relation exists. For directed valued graphs, the adjacency matrix would look like this:

	A	B	C	D	E
A	0	2	0	5	4
B	2	0	0	1	0
C	0	0	0	3	4
D	6	2	3	0	0
E	5	3	4	0	0

The major disadvantage of adjacency matrices is that cells with value = zero occupy the same size of memory that other cells occupy. In fact, over 90% of cells real social networks have value = zero. Therefore, adjacency matrices are difficult to make use of in practice, especially in the case of large networks.

Example:
Fortunately, the NetworkX library makes it easy to create, manipulate, and study the many aspects of complex networks and graphs. The main emphasis of it is to avoid the many complexities associated with the working of graph algorithms. In the

following example, we will show how we can create a basic adjacency matrix in NetworkX:

```
In:      import networkx as nx
         import 51atplotlib.pyplot as plt
         g = nx.cycle_graph(10)
         x = nx.adj_matrix(g)
         print(x.todense())
out:
         [[0 1 0 0 0 0 0 0 0 1]
          [1 0 1 0 0 0 0 0 0 0]
          [0 1 0 1 0 0 0 0 0 0]
          [0 0 1 0 1 0 0 0 0 0]
          [0 0 0 1 0 1 0 0 0 0]
          [0 0 0 0 1 0 1 0 0 0]
          [0 0 0 0 0 1 0 1 0 0]
          [0 0 0 0 0 0 1 0 1 0]
          [0 0 0 0 0 0 0 1 0 1]
          [1 0 0 0 0 0 0 0 1 0]]
```

There is another way to build the adjacency matrix with ten nodes, which is by creating a list of edges (pairs of node incidents):

```
In:      n = 10
         adj_mat = [(i, (i+1)%n) for i in range(n)]
         adj_mat += [(i,(i+2)%n) for i in range(n)]
         g = nx.Graph(adj_mat)
```

We can either specify the nodes' positions explicitly, or we can define an algorithm that can automatically compute the layout. In the following example, we will call the draw_circular() method that positions the nodes linearly on a circle (Fig. 2.2):

```
In:      nx.draw_networkx(g)
```

2.8.2 Edge List Matrix

Edge lists appeared as a solution to the sparsity problem in the adjacency matrices. In this type of graphs, what is needed is to list the vertices that each edge is incident to. Traversing the matrix also gives the graph vertices because the vertex is incident with at least one edge. However, in this type of data representation, size can grow linearly with the number of edges:

Fig. 2.2 Circular
representation of an
adjacency matrix

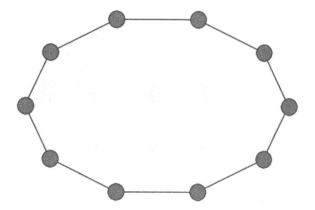

From	To	Value
A	B	1
A	D	4
A	E	5
B	A	3
C	E	3
D	A	5
E	C	1

The edge list matrices (or simply edge lists) are represented in python in the follow-ing way:

```
edge_list = {{'A','B', 1}, {'A','D', 4}, {'A','E',5}...}
```

Continuing our previous example, and rather than describing a graph as a collec-tion of nodes, we can alternatively describe it as a collection of edges that can also be associated with attributes:

Example:

```
In:   nx.to_edgelist(g)
Out: [(1, 2, {}), (1, 4, {}), (2, 3, {}), (3, 4, {})]
```

Because so for when we built our graph, we provided no attributes to the edges. Hence, the empty curly brackets ({}) represent empty attributes (such as distance, frequency, and so on).

2.8.3   Adjacency List

Although edge lists significantly mitigated the problem of small memory and data sparsity, they are not fast enough for search or traversal through graphs. To give even a better solution, adjacency lists were introduced: a list of links whose element "i → j" shows a link going from node i to node j (also represented as " i → {j₁, j₂, j₃, ...} "). In this type of data representation, the search is fast. Also, adding or removing nodes/edges is easy. Example:

From	Edges
A	(B 1), (D 4), (E 5)
...	

In Python, it is given in the following way:

```
edge_list = {'A':{'B':1, 'D':4, 'E':5}, 'B':{'A':3},...}
```

Example 1

```
In:  g = nx.Graph()
     g.add_edge(1,2)
     g.add_nodes_from([3,4])
     g.add_edge(3,4)
     g.add_edges_from([(2,3), (4,1)])
```

Now, let's draw the graph (Fig. 2.3):

```
In:  nx.draw_networkx(g, node_color='orange', node_size=400)
Out:
```

```
In:  g.nodes()
Out: [1, 2, 3, 4]
In:  g.edges()
Out: [(1, 2), (1, 4), (2, 3), (3, 4)]
```

We can describe this graph as an adjacency list by listing the neighbors of every node. For examples, the neighbors of node 1 are [2, 4] and the neighbors of node 2 are [1, 3], and so on.

```
In:  g.adjacency_list()
Out: [[2, 4], [1, 3], [2, 4], [1, 3]]
```

We can also represent this graph as a dictionary of lists in which the dictionary's keys are the nodes' names, and the dictionary's values are the nodes' adjacency lists. This type of representation makes it clear about the neighbors of each node.

Fig. 2.3 Simple graph
with four nodes

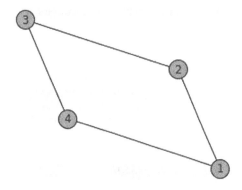

Fig. 2.4 ladder graph in
NetworkX

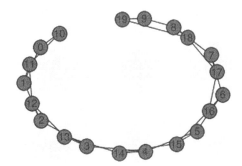

```
In:  nx.to_dict_of_lists(g)
Out:{1: [2, 4], 2: [1, 3], 3: [2, 4], 4: [1, 3]}
```

Example 2

We can also get the adjacency list of one of the NetworkX built-in networks
(Fig. 2.4):

```
In:  g = nx.ladder_graph(10)
     nx.draw_networkx(g)
Out:

In:  print(g.adjacency_list())
Out:
     [[1, 10], [0, 2, 11], [1, 3, 12], [2, 4, 13], [3, 5, 14],
     [4, 6, 15], [16, 5, 7], [8, 17, 6], [9, 18, 7], [8, 19],
     [0, 11], [1, 10, 12], [2, 11, 13], [3, 12, 14], [4, 13,
     15], [16, 5, 14], [17, 6, 15], [16, 18, 7], [8, 17, 19],
     [9, 18]]
```

Or if we want to print it as a dictionary of lists:

```
In:  print(nx.to_dict_of_lists(g))
Out:
     {0: [1, 10], 1: [0, 2, 11], 2: [1, 3, 12], 3: [2, 4, 13], 4: [3, 5,
     14], 5: [4, 6, 15], 6: [16, 5, 7], 7: [8, 17, 6], 8: [9, 18, 7], 9:
     [8, 19], 10: [0, 11], 11: [1, 10, 12], 12: [2, 11, 13], 13: [3, 12,
     14], 14: [4, 13, 15], 15: [16, 5, 14], 16: [17, 6, 15], 17: [16, 18,
     7], 18: [8, 17, 19], 19: [9, 18]}
```

2.8.4 Numpy Matrix

This type of matrices is exclusive to Python programming language. The matrix will contain one if there is a link between two nodes like i and j. Otherwise, it would contain 0.

```
In:  nx.to_numpy_matrix(g)
Out: matrix([[ 0.,   1.,   0.,   1.],
     [1.,  0.,   1.,   0.],
     [0.,  1.,   0.,   1.],
     [1.,  0.,   1.,   0.]])
```

2.8.5 Sparse Matrix

Since matrices are usually sparse which means that they usually contain very few ones as opposed to the number of zeros, they can be represented in the form of SciPy matrix:

```
In:  print(nx.to_scipy_sparse_matrix(g))
Out:  (0, 1)       1
      (0, 3)       1
      (1, 0)       1
      (1, 2)       1
      (2, 1)       1
      (2, 3)       1
      (3, 0)       1
      (3, 2)       1
```

2.9 Basic Matrix Operations

Let's take a look at some of the basic matrix operations

- *Vocabulary*: the size of a matrix is defined as the number of rows and columns in the matrix. If a matrix has the same number of rows and columns, then it is square. Otherwise, it is rectangular. Each entry in a matrix is called a cell. For a square matrix, the main diagonal of the matrix consists of entries for which the index of the row is equal to the index of the column.

- *Matrix permutation*: Matrix permutation is the rearrangement of rows and columns in a matrix. This is done at times when network tie patterns are not clear until we permute both the rows and the columns of the matrix. Matrix permutation is necessary for the study of cohesive subgroups, construction of block models, and evaluation of fitness of block models.
- *Matrix transpose*: the transpose of a matrix is done by the interchange of rows and columns in the original matrix. Digraph matrix is not always identical to its transpose since the sociomatrix of a directional relation is not typically symmetric.
- *Matrix addition*: adding two matrices with the same size. This is done by summing up the elements in the corresponding cells of the two matrices.
- *Matrix subtraction*: subtracting two matrices with the same size which can be done by calculating the difference between the elements in the corresponding cells of the two matrices.
- *Matrix multiplication*: the product of two matrices. Matrix multiplication is critical in the study of SNA as it can be used to examine walks and reachability and is the basis for compounding relations in the analysis of relational algebra.

Although matrices have been used widely over the years to visualize networks, they are rarely used today for this purpose due to the small number of matrix entries that can be used in comparison with the large number of online networks entries that must be considered.

2.10 Data Visualization

Data visualization is very useful for network analysis since it helps users recognize the important structural features of the network visually.

A graph is the most meaningful way to visualize network data, particularly when the network size is enormous. Trees, undirected graphs in which every two vertices are connected by one simple path, are also used at some times for data visualization and particularly when the dataset is small. Trees can be polytree, rooted, labeled, recursive, directed, free, binary, or ternary.

Matrices are arrays of elements consisting of rows and columns, where the intersection between a column and a row is called the cell. Common types of matrices include column-matrices, row matrices, square matrices, identity matrices, diagonal matrices, symmetric matrices, skew-symmetric matrices, triangle matrices, and null matrices. In the study of social networks, the common types are adjacency matrices, edge list matrices, and adjacency list.

Other visualization tools include maps and hybrid approaches, multidimensional visualization techniques that used in both graphs and maps.

Chapter 3
Graph Theory

The chapter introduces the main features of graph theory, the mathematical study of the application, and properties of graphs, initially motivated by the study of games of chance. It addresses topics such as origins of graph theory, graph basics, types of graphs, graph traversals, and types of operations on graphs.

3.1 Origins of Graph Theory

The first article wrote on graph theory was in 1736 by Leonhard Euler, who studied the problem of the Seven Bridges of Königsberg (now Kaliningrad, Russia) of how to take a walk through the town by visiting each area of the town and crossing each bridge only once. Königsberg was a city in Prussia that time with the river Pregel flowed through the town, creating two islands. The city and the islands were connected by seven bridges as shown.

He had formulated an abstraction of the problem, eliminating unnecessary facts and focussing on the land areas and the bridges connecting them. He found out that the choice of a route inside each land area is irrelevant and that the only thing which mattered is the order in which the bridges are crossed. He discovered that this problem had no solution and that an eighth bridge is required to be built. Eulerian graphs are named after his name. His work, which gave birth to graph theory, is strongly connected to SNA (Fig. 3.1).

Freeman (2004) traced the first use of visual images back to Jacob Moreno (1932–1934), a psychologist, who used what is called "sociogram" (also known as the node-link diagram) as a method to represent the interpersonal structure of a group of people.

The use of graph theory in the study of social relations was commenced by a group of mathematicians and psychologists in the 1940s. Graph theory allows researchers to prove theorems and deduce testable statements. It depicts a social

© Springer International Publishing AG 2017
M.Z. Al-Taie, S. Kadry, *Python for Graph and Network Analysis*, Advanced
Information and Knowledge Processing, DOI 10.1007/978-3-319-53004-8_3

Fig. 3.1 Origin of graph theory

network as a model of a social system that consists of actors and the ties among them.

A graph is a mathematical object that describes relationships between items. It is a structure for modeling information. It consists of nodes that represent objects and edges that relate one node to another. Graph theory offers the tools needed to describe and visualize social compositions that consist of three or more actors. This led to having a new realization of the social composition, in which ties represent both the human action and the context for human action.

Graphs have become ubiquitous in computing, as they can represent different kinds of real-world relations: friends in a social network, website pages, cells in a neural network, and so on. They are also standard data structures in the study of computer science.

Graph theory has become useful in the study of social networks for several reasons:

1. *First*, it provides a vocabulary that can be used to label and denote many social structural properties.
2. *Second*, it provides the use of many mathematical operations and ideas that help quantify and measure many of the social structural properties.
3. *Third*, graph theory gives a way to prove theorems of graphs and representations of social structure.

Graphs are important in research because they provide abstractions to real life, represent information flows that exist, explicitly demonstrate relationships, enable computations across large datasets, and allow computing locally the areas of interest with small traversals.

Many practical problems can be represented as graphs. For example, they have been used to model problems or situations in physics, biology, psychology, and computer science. In computer science, graphs are used to represent networks of communication, data organization, computational devices, and the flow of computation. The link structure of websites can also be seen as a graph.

Graph algorithms (e.g., Bellman-Ford, Dijkstra, Ford-Fulkerson, Kruskai, nearest neighbor, depth-first search, and breadth-first search) have been designed to solve problems related to graph traversals, graph coloring, connected components, shortest paths, Hamiltonian paths, Eulerian paths, and the Traveling Salesman Problem.

With this in mind, classes of problems related to graph study fall into a few categories:

1. *Existence*: problems that attempt to determine if a path, a vertex, or a set exists, particularly if there is a constraint.
2. *Construction*: given a set of paths and vertices, and within given constraint, how to construct a graph?
3. *Enumeration*: problems that attempt to determine how many vertices and edges exist, given a set of constraints.
4. *Optimization*: problems that attempt to find the shortest path between two nodes.

3.2   Graph Basics

Simply, a graph is a set of points and lines that connect them. It is a way of representing the relationships among a collection of objects.

Points are called "vertices," and lines are called "edges." A graph G with a set X of vertices together with a set E of edges is written as $G=(X,E)$ (Fig. 3.2).

We suppose that in $G=(X,E)$, $x,y \in X$. The distance from x to y, denoted by $d(x,y)$, is the length of the shortest (x,y)-path. If there is no such path in G, then $d(x,y)=\infty$. In this case, G is disconnected, putting x and y in two different network parts. The diameter of G, denoted by $diam(G)$, is the distance between the farthest two vertices, or $\max_{x,y \in X} d(x,y)$.

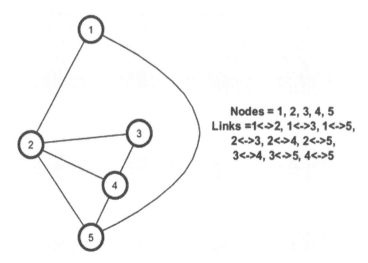

Nodes = 1, 2, 3, 4, 5
Links =1<->2, 1<->3, 1<->5,
2<->3, 2<->4, 2<->5,
3<->4, 3<->5, 4<->5

Fig. 3.2 Simple graph with five nodes and seven edges

A walk is an alternating sequence of vertices and edges where every edge connects the preceding vertex and the succeeding vertex in the sequence. Put simply; a walk is a list of links that are sequentially connected to form a continuous route. A walk starts at a vertex and ends at a vertex. It can be a trail, path, or cycle:

1. Trail is a walk that does not go through the same link more than once.
2. Path is a walk that does not go through the same node more than once.
3. The cycle is a walk that starts and ends at the same node and that does not go through the same node on its way.

A few final list of terms will help us in our discussion. A loop is an edge that connects a vertex to itself. Vertices with no neighbors (degree =0) are called isolated. Two vertices can be connected with more than one edge. Such edges are referred to as "parallel" or "multiple." An ordered pair of vertices is known as an "arc." If (x, y) is an arc, then x is called the initial vertex and y is called the terminal vertex.

3.3 Vertices

Vertices (or nodes) are the core elements of all graphs. They share the following characteristics:

- In a graph $G = (X, E)$ and a vertex $x \epsilon X$: The deletion of x from G means removing x from set X and removing all the edges that contain x. However, the removal of an edge is easier than that of a vertex, because the deletion of an edge requires only that the edge is removed from the list of edges.
- For a given vertex x, the number of all adjacent vertices is called "degree" and denoted by $d(x)$. The maximum degree over all vertices is known as the highest degree of G. Adjacent vertices are sometimes called neighbors, and the set of neighbors of a given vertex x is referred to as the neighborhood of x, denoted by $N(x)$. The set of edges incident to a vertex x is denoted by $E(x)$ (Fig. 3.3).

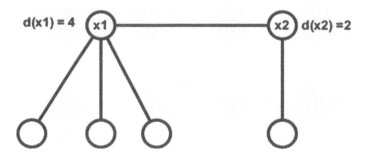

Fig. 3.3 Degree of vertices

- The degree of a vertex is the number of edges incident to it. An isolated vertex is a vertex with degree zero, that is, a vertex which is not the endpoint of any edge. A leaf vertex is a vertex of degree one.
- The two vertices that are connected by an edge are called its endpoints. The edge is described as the incident with the vertices. A simple adjacency between two vertices means there is exactly one edge between them.
- In a directed graph, the out-degree measure is the number of outgoing edges, while the in-degree measure is the number of incoming edges. A source vertex is a vertex with in-degree zero, while a sink vertex is a vertex without-degree zero.
- A cut-vertex is a vertex that if removed, the number of network components increases. A vertex-separator is a collection of vertices that if removed, the graph would be disassembled into small components.
- A labeled vertex is a vertex that is associated with a value that adds further information to the labeled vertex.

3.4   Types of Graphs

There are several different types of graphs in graph theory to represent the relationship between nodes. The most common of which are:

1. *Undirected graph*: a graph having edges with no direction. This type of graphs is used to represent symmetric links. For instance, if two people (two nodes in a network) shake hands at some place (are connected to each other), this gives the feeling that the relation is mutual (undirected). Facebook friendships and LinkedIn connections require mutual confirmation which is forced by the system regulations. The reason is that when person "A" shakes hand with person "B," person B shakes hand with person A as well. Undirected graphs can be easily transformed to directed graphs by giving direction to edges (Fig. 3.4).
2. *Directed graph*: also called digraph, is a graph having edges with direction. This notion can be better realized if we imagine, for example, that Alice knows Bob, but the opposite is not true. Teacher-student or boss-employee relationships are assumed to be asymmetric. In the context of graph theory, this can be depicted as a directed edge from Bob to Alice. Another possible example is the field of wireless networking where the link between two different nodes can be asymmetric if messages can only be sent in one direction (Fig. 3.5).
3. *Weighted graph*: graphs having weights of real values associated with the edges. Edge weights may represent a concept such as connection cost, length, capacity, similarity, distance, etc., which depends on the specific use of that graph. For example, when modeling a railway network as a graph, railway stations are represented as vertices, while edges connect adjacent stations. Weights can be added here to the edges to give the distance between every two stations. The weight of the graph is calculated as the sum of the weights associated with all edges. Another useful example is the frequency of communication in a relationship

Fig. 3.4 Undirected graph

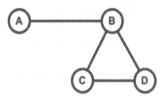

Fig. 3.5 Directed graph

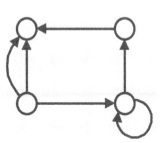

which was found to reflect accurately on the emotional content and amount of influence. Low frequency of communication (also known as weak ties) between two people requires little or no personal time and energy to maintain. This means that they are desynchronized in what they receive and when, although such a model of communication can at times be significant such that the information that passes is usually novel and comes from a different point of view (Fig. 3.6).

4. *Planar graph*: a graph in a two-dimensional plane with no crossing between ties. Planarity can be substantial. For example, when designing transportation networks, a planar graph here means that there is no need to include bridges or tunnels in the design. Another example is the design of electrical circuits, which connect chips, requires that the wires that connect the different components should not cross each other. One way to achieve this is by putting chips in different layers where each layer, in this case, is a planar graph by itself (Fig. 3.7).
5. *Orthogonal graph*: a graph having horizontal and vertical lines.
6. *Grid-based graph*: a graph in which vertices and edges are placed on a two-dimensional grid.

There are also other types of graphs that display data in a different way:

1. *Simple graph.* A simple graph is an undirected graph with no loops or multi-edge connecting between any two vertices. Each edge connects a pair of distinct vertices.
2. *Regular graph.* A regular (or uniform) graph is a graph in which all vertices have the same number of neighbors, which is the degree of each vertex (Fig. 3.8).
3. *Complete graph.* A graph in which any pair of nodes are connected (often written as K1, K2, …) (Fig. 3.9).

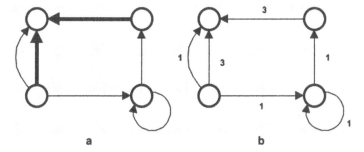

Fig. 3.6 Two ways to show the strength of a relationship

Fig. 3.7 Planar graph

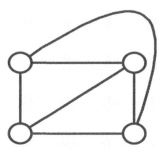

Fig. 3.8 Regular graph

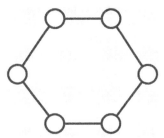

4. *Mixed graph*. A mixed graph G is a graph in which some edges are directed, and other edges are undirected. Directed and undirected graphs are special cases.
5. *Multigraph*. The term multigraph is used to point out that multiple edges (and sometimes loops) are used in a particular type of graphs.
6. *Half-edges, loose edges graph*. It is a graph with only one end that is called half-edges or no ends (loose edges). Examples include signed graphs and biased graphs.
7. *Finite and infinite graphs*. A finite graph is a graph $G=(V,E)$ in which V and E are finite sets. An infinite graph is a graph with an infinite set of vertices, edges, or both.

Fig. 3.9 Complete graph

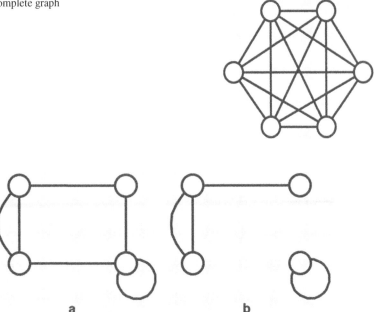

Fig. 3.10 (**a**) connected graph, (**b**) disconnected graph

8. *Connected and disconnected graph.* A graph is called connected if every pair of distinct vertices in this graph is connected; otherwise, it is called disconnected (Fig. 3.10).
9. *K-vertex-connected graph.* A graph is called k-vertex-connected or k-edge-connected if there is no k-1 vertices (respectively, edges) disconnecting the graph. A k-vertex-connected graph is often simply called k-connected.
10. *Weakly and strongly connected graph.* A directed graph is called weakly connected if the replacement of all of the directed edges with undirected edges produces a connected (undirected) graph. A graph is strongly connected (or strong) if it contains a directed path from u to v and a directed path from v to u for every pair of vertices u, v.

3.5 Graph Traversals

Most network analysis tools iterate through a graph (i.e., over its nodes and edges) and calculating some quantity of interest. The goal can be finding the shortest path between two points, finding connected clusters, or calculating node and edge betweenness. In some cases, the goal is to walk the entire network to understand it or to sample the network data. In any case, all these techniques require the implementation of one of the traversal algorithms that were designed to either find

Fig. 3.11 Depth-first
search traversal

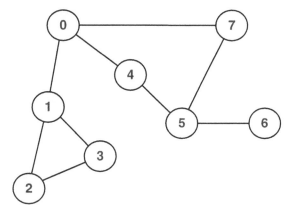

shortest paths between points or to walk across the graph and try to understand its
structure.

3.5.1   Depth-First Traversal (DFS)

Depth-first traversal is a uninformed search technique that systematically traverses
nodes until it finds its goal (Fig. 3.11). The algorithm traverses down a child's child
and then backtracks to each of its siblings, which finally produces a spanning tree of
the nodes it has visited. The edges that lead to the newly discovered nodes are maintained as "discovery edges," and the edges that are used for backtracking are maintained as "back edges." The two types of edges along with visited nodes establish
what is called the spanning tree. There is also an iterative version of the standard
algorithm that has a stack to maintain visited nodes.

Example
Let's try the DFS algorithm with NetworkX using one of the simple graphs in
NetworkX. This implementation is based on the work of D. Eppstein (July 2004)
(Fig. 3.12).

```
In:   g = nx.barabasi_albert_graph(10, 5)
      print(nx.info(g))
```

```
In:   edges = nx.dfs_edges(g, 0)
```

We let DFS know where to start graph traversing by providing the source node,
which in this case it is 0.

Fig. 3.12 Barabasi-Albert
graph in NetworkX

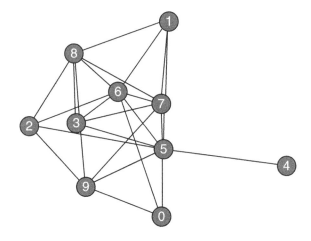

```
In:   print(edges)
Out:  <generator object dfs_edges at 0x000000000A742318>
```

Printing the edges object alone produces the object generator, which is a Python construct for lazy evaluation. However, we can turn around this by using the list function from Python as follows:

```
In:   print(list(edges))
Out:  [(0, 9), (9, 8), (8, 1), (1, 5), (5, 2), (2, 6), (6, 3),
       (3, 7), (5, 4)]
```

Let's produce the list of nodes embedded in the graph as a list:

```
In: print(list(nx.dfs_tree(g,0)))
Out: [0, 1, 2, 3, 4, 5, 6, 7, 8, 9]
```

Let's also use the tree function which will return oriented tree constructed from a DFS from source:

```
In:   tree = nx.dfs_tree(g, 0)
      print(list(tree.edges()))
Out:  [(0, 9), (1, 5), (2, 6), (3, 7), (5, 2), (5, 4), (6, 3),
       (8, 1), (9, 8)]
```

Here is how the DFS tree looks. A bold edge represents the arrow head (Fig. 3.13).

```
In:   nx.draw_networkx(tree)
Out:
```

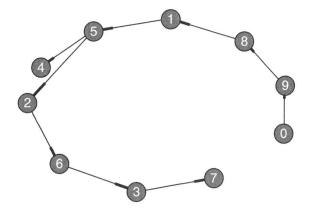

Fig. 3.13 Depth-first search algorithm in a treelike structure

The dfs_successors function will return a dictionary with nodes as keys and list of successor nodes as values:

```
In:   successors = nx.dfs_successors(g, 0)\
      print(successors)
Out:
      {0: [9], 1: [5], 2: [6], 3: [7], 5: [2, 4], 6: [3], 8:
      [1], 9: [8]}
```

While the dfs_predecessors function will return a dictionary with nodes as keys and predecessor nodes as values:

```
In:   predecessors = nx.dfs_predecessors(g, 0)
      print(predecessors)
Out:  {1: 8, 2: 5, 3: 6, 4: 5, 5: 1, 6: 2, 7: 3, 8: 9, 9: 0}
```

3.5.2 Breadth-First Traversal (BFS)

This algorithm traverses the network by finding the shortest path from a single-source vertex(s) to every other vertex in the same network segment. It involves iterating through the neighbors of all the nodes in the current shell and adding to the next shell all subsequent neighbors who have not already been visited. In this way, the algorithm can calculate the shortest distance between two nodes. Breadth-first search can also discover, with minor modifications, if there is more than one geodesic path between two nodes.

The way that breadth-first search algorithm applies to find shortest paths is as follows: we know only that "s" has distance 0 from itself while distances to all other vertices are unknown. Next, we find all the neighbors of "s," which by definition

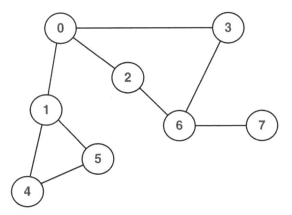

Fig. 3.14 Breadth-first
search traversal

have distance one from "s," followed by finding the neighbors of these vertices. Excluding those already visited, these vertices must have distance two from "s" and their neighbors, except those already visited, have distance "3" and so on (Fig. 3.14).

Here, we are going to follow the same steps that we applied in the DFS section using the Barabasi-Albert graph implementation in NetworkX:

```
In:  edges = nx.bfs_edges(g, 0)
     print(list(edges))
Out: [(0, 8), (0, 9), (0, 5), (0, 6), (0, 7), (8, 3), (9, 1),
     (5, 2), (5, 4)]

In:  print(list(nx.bfs_tree(g,0)))
Out: [0, 1, 2, 3, 4, 5, 6, 7, 8, 9]
```

Let's define the BFS tree:

```
In:  tree = nx.bfs_tree(g, 0)
     print(list(tree.edges()))
Out: [(0, 8), (0, 9), (0, 5), (0, 6), (0, 7), (5, 2), (5, 4),
     (8, 3), (9, 1)]
```

As we can see, the search tree in BFS is different from what it was when we performed the DFS search algorithm.

Let's draw the BFS tree (Fig. 3.15):

```
In:  nx.draw_networkx(tree)
Out:
```

Next, we calculate the successors and predecessors:

Fig. 3.15 Breadth-first
search algorithm in a
treelike structure

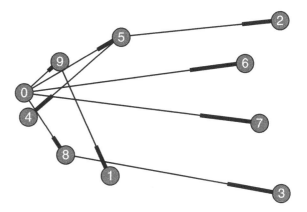

```
In:  successors = nx.bfs_successors(g,0)
     print(successors)
Out: {0: [8, 9, 5, 6, 7], 8: [3], 5: [2, 4], 9: [1]}

In:  predecessors = nx.bfs_predecessors(g,0)
     print(predecessors)
Out: {1: 9, 2: 5, 3: 8, 4: 5, 5: 0, 6: 0, 7: 0, 8: 0, 9: 0}
```

As we expected, the BFS dictionary of lists for both successors and predecessors
is different from what we saw in the DFS case, which points out that each algorithm
followed its way traversing the Barabasi-Albert graph (and also any other graph).

3.5.3 Dijkstra's Algorithm

This algorithm was published by Edsger Dijkstra in 1959 and is one of the most
important algorithms in modern communication networks and the base of many so-
called routing algorithms that are used on the Internet. Dijkstra's algorithm finds the
shortest path from a given node to every other node in the same network by considering the length of edges. This is done by keeping a record of the shortest path the
algorithm has found so far while this record is updated whenever a new shorter path
is found. At the end of the implementation, the shortest distance to each vertex is
determined.

Example
NetworkX also has a nice implementation of Dijkstra's algorithm.

We are going to draw a simple graph and see the implementation of some of the
functions (Fig. 3.16).

```
In:  g = nx.watts_strogatz_graph(0.5 ,2 ,20)
     nx.draw_networkx(g)
Out:
```

Fig. 3.16 Watts-Strogatz
graph with 20 nodes

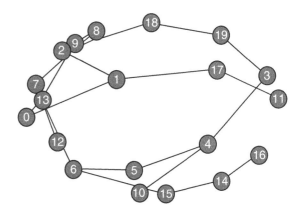

```
In:    print(nx.info(g))
Out:

       Name: watts_strogatz_graph(20,2,0.5)
       Type: Graph
       Number of nodes: 20
       Number of edges: 20
       Average degree:    2.0000
```

Let's see more details about the Watts-Strogatz graph:

```
In:    nx.watts_strogatz_graph?
Out:
Signature:
nx.watts_strogatz_graph(n, k, p, seed=None)
Docstring:
Return a Watts-Strogatz small-world graph.


Parameters
----------
n : int
    The number of nodes
k : int
    Each node is joinedwith its ``k`` nearest neighbors in a ring
    topology.
p : float
    The probability of rewiring each edge
seed : int, optional
    Seed for random number generator (default=None)


...
```

The nx.dijkstra_path function returns the distance between any two points in a graph. The function takes as input the starting point, the ending point, and weight (optional) and returns a list of nodes in the shortest path:

```
In:   nx.dijkstra_path(g, 0, 15)
Out:  [0, 2, 1, 17, 18, 15]
```

We can also find the length of this path by using the nx.dijkstra_path_length function. The function takes as input a source node and a target node, in addition to weight which is optional. The function returns an integer which is the shortest path length.

```
In:   nx.dijkstra_path_length(g, 0, 15)
Out:  5
```

Let's take a look at the list of nodes that consist the Wattss-Strogatz graph:

```
In:  print(g.nodes())
Out: [0, 1, 2, 3, 4, 5, 6, 7, 8, 9, 10, 11, 12, 13, 14, 15,
      16, 17, 18, 19, 20, 21, 22, 23, 24, 25, 26, 27, 28, 29,
      30, 31, 32, 33]
```

The itertools.combinations() function from the itertools package allows us to see the paths available in the graph. The second argument specifies the length of paths returned by the function:

```
In:  import itertools
In:  print(list(itertools.combinations(g.nodes(), 3)))
Out:
     [(0, 1, 2), (0, 1, 3), (0, 1, 4), (0, 1, 5), (0, 1, 6), (0, 1, 7),
      (0, 1, 8), (0, 1, 9), (0, 1, 10), (0, 1, 11), (0, 1, 12), (0, 1, 13),
      (0, 1, 14),…]
```

We can alternatively limit the number of results from the above function by allowing only for a small number of nodes (say 5):

```
In:   print(list(itertools.combinations(g.nodes()[:5], 3)))
Out:  [(0, 1, 2), (0, 1, 3), (0, 1, 4), (0, 2, 3), (0, 2, 4),
      (0, 3, 4), (1, 2, 3), (1, 2, 4), (1, 3, 4), (2, 3, 4)]
```

3.6   Operations on Graphs

It is possible to produce new graphs from old graphs using one of the following methods:

1. *Elementary operations*: also called editing operations, elementary operations create new graphs via making local changes to network structure such as adding or deleting vertices (or edges), merging or splitting vertices, and so on.
2. *Graph rewrite operations*: replacing the occurrence of some pattern graph within the host graph by an instance of the corresponding replacement graph.
3. *Unary operations*: creating an entirely new graph from an old one. Examples include line graph, dual graph, and complement graph.
4. *Binary operations*: creating a new graph from two parent graphs. Examples of binary operations include the disjoint union of graphs, Cartesian product of graphs, the tensor product of graphs, a strong product of graphs, and lexicographic product of graphs.

Reference

Freeman LC (2004) The development of social network analysis: a study in the sociology of science. BookSurge, LLC, North Charleston

Chapter 4
Social Networks

This chapter introduces the main concepts of social networks such as properties of social networks, data collection in social networks, data sampling, and social network analysis.

4.1 Social Networks

A social network is a social composition of actors and relationship defined on them. Actors can be persons, places, organizations, roles, etc., while a relationship can be kinship, friendship, knowledge, acquaintance, correspondence, etc. Every actor in the network can be connected to one or more other actors to form eventually a structure that represents the social tissue for that individual. We can think of a social network as a map of ties between the nodes that are investigated by analysts. Almost, any system in which humans participate and communicate can be considered a social network.

Network nodes mostly represent persons or organizations. However, they can also refer to Web pages, journal articles, departments, neighborhoods, or even countries (Marin and Wellman 2010). The enormous interest in the study of social networks today comes as a result of the expected benefit from investigating the research questions surrounding social networks as well as the challenges associated with data collection and network analysis.

Ties that connect actors in a network can be directed (to indicate the source and destination of a relationship) or undirected (to indicate a reciprocated relationship). Ties can also be dichotomous (to indicate the presence or absence of the relationship) or valued (measured on a specific scale) (Borgatti and Foster 2003).

Social networks can be grouped into two types: one mode and multimode. One-mode networks are those that include one type of nodes to represent actors (usually people), subgroups, or communities. The relations among nodes in these networks can represent individual evaluation (such as friendship), transfer of materials (such

© Springer International Publishing AG 2017
M.Z. Al-Taie, S. Kadry, *Python for Graph and Network Analysis*, Advanced
Information and Knowledge Processing, DOI 10.1007/978-3-319-53004-8_4

as borrowing or buying), transferring of non-materials (such as communication), interactions, formal roles, or kinship (such as marriage).

The second type of social networks, which is two-mode networks, includes two different sets of nodes. People possess information and resource, investors buy stock in corporations or companies employ people, and many others are all examples of 2-mode or bimodal networks.

Most of the networks are one-mode, but some certain problems require the analysis of two types of nodes (such as organizations and organization members, or events and people attending the event) (Marin and Wellman 2010).

4.2   Properties of a Social Network

4.2.1   Scale-Free Networks

Scale-free networks are networks whose degree distribution obeys a power law $P(k) \sim K^{-\gamma}$ (i.e., a few well-connected nodes, a lot of poorly connected nodes). Degree distribution is calculated as follows:

$$P_k = \frac{1}{n} \# \{i | k_i = k\}$$

Many networks including citation networks, biological networks, WWW graph, Internet graph, and social networks have right-skewed or power-law degree distribution (Fig. 4.1).

Power-law distribution means that few nodes account for the vast majority of links, while most nodes have very few links, which emphasizes the idea that we have a core with a periphery of nodes with few connections.

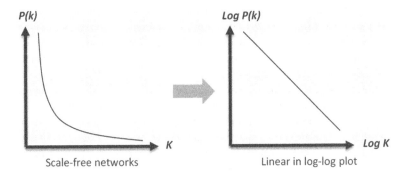

Fig. 4.1 Power-law degree distribution of scale-free networks

In these networks, a small number of well-connected nodes (hubs) significantly reduce the diameter of the entire networks. Such degree-distribution seems to be dynamically formed and maintained by quite simple, self-organizing mechanisms.

```
In:    import networkx as nx
       g = nx.scale_free_graph(40, alpha=0.41, beta=0.54, gamma=0.05,
       delta_in=0.2, delta_out=0, create_using=None, seed=None)
```

The nx.scale_free_graph function takes the following parameters:

- n (integer) – Number of nodes in the graph.
- alpha (float) – Probability for adding a new node connected to an existing node chosen randomly according to the in-degree distribution.
- beta (float) – Probability for adding an edge between two existing nodes. One existing node is chosen randomly according to the in-degree distribution and the other chosen randomly according to the out-degree distribution.
- gamma (float) – Probability for adding a new node connected to an existing node chosen randomly according to the out-degree distribution.
- delta_in (float) – Bias for choosing nodes from in-degree distribution.
- delta_out (float) – Bias for choosing nodes from out-degree distribution.
- create_using (graph, optional (default MultiDiGraph)) – Use this graph instance to start the process (default = 3-cycle).
- seed (integer, optional) – Seed for random number generator.

The function returns a scale-free directed graph (Fig. 4.2).

```
In:    print(nx.info(g))
Out:   Name:
           directed_scale_free_graph(40,alpha=0.41,beta=0.54,gamma=0.05,delta
           _in=0.2,delta_out=0)
           Type: MultiDiGraph
           Number of nodes: 40
           Number of edges: 78
           Average in degree:    1.9500
           Average out degree:   1.9500
In:    plt.figure(figsize=(8,8))
           layout = nx.spring_layout(g)
           nx.draw_networkx(g, layout=layout, with_labels=True,
           node_size=800, node_color='yellow')
```

4.2.2   Small-World Networks

In small-world networks, most nodes are homogeneous and can be reached by a small number of steps. This means that each node has roughly the same number of links, and the distance between any two nodes grows proportionally to the logarithm

Fig. 4.2 Directed
scale-free graph with 40
nodes

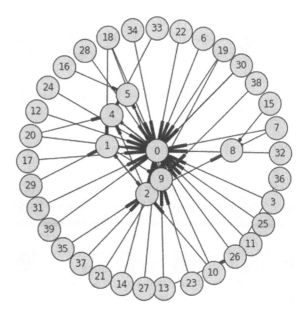

of the order of the network. Typically, small-world networks have many local links
and few long-range "shortcuts." They have high clustering coefficient, short average
path length, and over-abundance of hub nodes. They consist of dense communities
or clusters that are loosely connected by boundary spanners (also called connec-
tors). Even though these networks are uniform, they decay exponentially.

NetworkX has a nice implementation for small-world networks. One of the famous
graphs in this category is Watts-Strogatz(WS) small-world graph. The function returns
a Watts-Strogatz small-world graph and accepts three parameters: n (int) which is the
number of nodes, k (in) where each node is connected to k nearest neighbors in a ring
topology, and seed (optional int) for random number generator (default = none).

The way that WS graphs are generated is as follows: First, create a ring of n
nodes. Then each node in the ring is connected with its k nearest neighbors (k-1
neighbors if k is odd). Then shortcuts are created by replacing some edges as follows: for each edge u-v in the underlying "n-ring with k nearest neighbors" with
probability p, replace it with a new edge u-w with uniformly random choice of
existing node w (Fig. 4.3).

```
In:      Import networkx as nx
             g = nx.watts_strogatz_graph(25, 5, 0.4)
             print(nx.info(g))
Out:     Name: watts_strogatz_graph(25,5,0.4)
           Type: Graph
           Number of nodes: 25
           Number of edges: 50
           Average degree:   4.0000
In:      nx.draw_networkx(g, node_color='c', node_size=300)
Out:
```

Fig. 4.3 Watts-Strogatz
small-world graph with 25
nodes

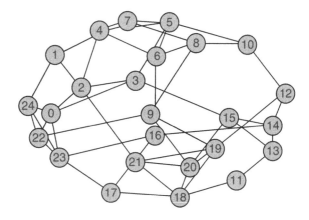

4.2.3   Network Navigation

Network navigation means that besides the small-world phenomenon, people are good at finding paths in networks.

4.2.4   Dunbar's Number

Robin Dunbar suggested a cognitive limit to the number of individuals with whom one can maintain stable social relationships. These are relationships in which an actor knows who each person is and how each person relates to every other person. It has been proposed to lie between 100 and 250, with a commonly used value of 150. Dunbar's number states the number of people one knows and keeps social contact with, and it does not include the number of people known personally with a ceased social relationship, nor people just generally known with a lack of persistent social relationship, a number which might be much higher and likely depends on long-term memory.

4.3   Data Collection in Social Networks

One of the characteristics of social networks is that data are grounded in cultural values and symbols and are formed through motives, meanings, and typifications.

The implementation of SNA techniques requires either a complete dataset (which is not always available) or a sample dataset that is extracted from the complete set, where inference about the population can be made later based on the sample.

Researchers are used to collecting data using traditional methods such as questionnaires, interviews, observations, and archival records, while online data can be collected mainly using APIs, Web crawlers, online surveys, and specialized applications.

Collecting social network data would allow us to answer questions like: what can we learn about responders? Is there any demographic data associated with them? What kind of quantitative metrics (e.g., centrality) can be derived from the data? Moreover, what kind of quantitative and qualitative outcomes (e.g., the ability to become a good citizen) can we measure?

Many network data collection methods have been developed over the years where the goal always is to find the ties between actors in the network, even though data, data management, and data analysis tools used in each method may be different. At times, researchers need to use more than one method to gather actor attribute information. Traditional methods to collect social data include (Wasserman and Faust 1994, p. 43):

1. *Questionnaires*. This is the most common method of data collection. They are particularly useful in settings where the respondents can report on the relations to be studied. A questionnaire typically contains questions about whether the respondent has ties to the other actors. Questionnaires are also useful in cases where the respondents work for some corporation since they can report on a group of ties such as the people whom they like to eat with, respect, go out with, or ask for advice. The questionnaire design can be roster vs. free call, free vs. fixed choice, and ratings vs. complete rankings.
2. *Interviews*. Interviews are used to gather network data either by face-to-face communications, over the telephone, or by any other means. They are more used when the use of questionnaires does not provide the desired results.
3. *Observation*. Social network data can be collected by monitoring the different interactions between actors. This method has been used to study relatively small groups of people where face-to-face interviews are not feasible. They are widely used to monitor the behavior and interactions of people in different settings and also of nonhuman primates such as monkeys.
4. *Archival records*. In this method, collecting data is done through examining measurements taken from past interaction records. Records can be political interactions between nations, scholar-scholar citation records, journal articles, newspapers, court records, meetings, and so on. The importance of this method is that data can give rise to the longitudinal relations, which can be used to reconstruct the ties that existed in the past.
5. *Other*. Other possible data collection methods include the cognitive, social structure design, experimental studies, as well as the studies that are targeted to collect ego-network data since they are usually used to estimate the size or composition of an individual's ego-centered network.

4.4   Six Degrees of Separation

In 1969, a psychologist called Stanley Milgram did an experiment (later named after his name: Milgram Experiment) of sending out 300 letters to some randomly selected addresses in Nebraska and Kansas. Each of the 300 letters had instructions on how to deliver the letter back to Boston through a series of acquaintances. Only 64 letters, out of 300, arrived their destination with an average chain length of 5.5.

4.5   Online Social Networks

Online social networks or social media websites—the recent form of traditional social networks—have several mechanisms that allow people to comprehend, interact, engage, and collaborate with each other. Platforms such as Facebook, YouTube, LinkedIn, and Twitter are used these days heavily either for fun or business processes. You can provide your feedback or share your experiences with the one you choose. Many businesses have recognized the importance and quality of the end services offered by social media.

4.6   Online Social Data Collection

In the past, social data was very difficult to collect and hard to come by, and many people in the field limited their study to only small standard sets of data and never risked to build their datasets. However, things have changed with the advent of online social data sources such as Twitter, Facebook, and Flicker that generate much more data than anyone would expect.

Online social networks allow users to share text, audio, video, hyperlinks, and photographs with others. They store large volumes of personal data, which not only can provide information about the users themselves but also show their online social activities. For example, Facebook stores more than 30 billion new pieces of content every month, produced by more than one billion active users. Beyond the traditional methods of collecting social data, online data can be collected by the following methods:

1. *APIs*. The use of APIs that are provided by the OSN services. Such use includes sending queries to the website with the help of API to collect data.
2. *Web crawlers*. This method includes building a Web crawler to crawl the website. The crawler uses HTTP requests/responses to collect data from the website.
3. *Online surveys*. Online surveys collect user activities by asking them about how, when, and with whom they would share content.
4. *Deployed applications*. In this method, a custom application is deployed to collect content from the website. This approach is more flexible regarding monitoring user behavior in situ and collecting the data that users do not share online.

Nevertheless, all network data collection methods suffer from some drawbacks, particularly about information accuracy, information validity, information reliability, and measurement error (Wasserman and Faust 1994, p. 56).

4.7 Data Sampling

In some cases, taking measurements on all actors in the relevant actor set is not possible. Therefore, taking a sample set of actors from the complete set becomes enough, and inference about the population is made later based on the sample. Sampled data in this case, which can be viewed as representative of the larger population, is called the probability sample.

Several sampling techniques have been developed. The three most frequently techniques used here are:

1. *Node sampling*. In this method, a limited subset of nodes alongside their links are chosen to be the sampled data.
2. *Link sampling*. In this approach, a subset of links is selected to represent the sampled data.
3. *Snowball sampling*. This method starts with a set of sampled nodes alongside their neighbors. These nominated nodes are the first-order zone of the network. Next, the nodes in this zone are sampled, and all their connections are extracted to form the second-order zone. This process is done several times and leads eventually have a network of several zones.

One of the simplest methods is called snowball sampling (also known as chain sampling or respondent-driven sampling.) Collecting sample data starts with a set of sampled respondents who report on the actors with whom they have a connection. Nominated actors represent the first-order zone of the network. Next, the actors in this zone are sampled, and all their connections are extracted, which is going to form the second-order zone. This process is repeated several times to have a network with several zones.

A typical implementation of the algorithm requires that we limit the depth of search to a predetermined number to avoid issues like the explosion of data that the snowball sampling method can deliver and the human limit of perception of social networks (also known as horizon of observability).

The following snowball sampling example gives credits to "Social Network Analysis for Startups" book. It uses data from a website called LiveJournal which is very popular in Russia and Eastern Europe.

The function below fetches a list of friends of the username from the API walks through the lines in the response and add edges. It takes two arguments: a graph object and a string seed. The function collects data for a given node.

```
In:    import sys
       import os
       import networkx as nx
       import urllib
In:
       def read_lj_friends(g, name):
           # fetch the friend-list from LiveJournal
       response=urllib.urlopen('http://www.livejournal.com/misc/fdata.bml?
       user='+name)
           for line in response.readlines():
               #Comments in the response start with a '#'
               if line.startswith('#'): continue

               # the format is "< name" (incoming) or "> name" (outgoing)
               parts=line.split()

               #make sure that we do not have an empty line
               if len(parts)==0: continue

               #add the edge to the network
               if parts[0]=='<':
                   g.add_edge(parts[1],name)
               else:
                   g.add_edge(name,parts[1])
```

The following Python code implements snowball sampling over data collected
from LiveJournal. The function takes two required arguments: a graph object and
the name of a central node. The optional argument max_depth assigns the depth to
which the digging process should go (the default value is 1).

```
In:
       def snowball_sampling(g, center, max_depth=1, current_depth=0,
       taboo_list=[]):
           # if we have reached the depth limit of the search, bomb out.
           print center, current_depth, max_depth, taboo_list
           if current_depth==max_depth:
               print 'out of depth'
               return taboo_list
           if center in taboo_list:
               print 'taboo'
               return taboo_list #we've been here before
           else:
               taboo_list.append(center) # we shall never return

           read_lj_friends(g, center)

           for node in g.neighbors(center):
               taboo_list=snowball_sampling(g, node,
       current_depth=current_depth+1, max_depth=max_depth,
       taboo_list=taboo_l ist)

           return taboo_list
```

We will define a graph object, g = net. Graph(), that the function will fill in with nodes and edges. We will also pass the username of the person (in this case valerois), whose friendship network should be sampled, to the snowball_sampling() function which in turn will invoke the read_lj_friends() function to collect the required data.

```
In:     g=net.Graph()
        snowball_sampling(g,'valerois')
Out:
        valerois 0 1 []
        zhabaevent 1 1 ['valerois']
        out of depth
        farbys 1 1 ['valerois']
        out of depth
        zlove 1 1 ['valerois']
        out of depth
        cute_n_gorgeous 1 1 ['valerois']
        out of depth
        st_shtuchka 1 1 ['valerois']
        out of depth
        vorodis 1 1 ['valerois']
        ........
```

To save the result of snowball sampling in a pajek format:

```
In:     net.write_pajek(g, "LiveJournaData.net")
```

To open the file in NetworkX, the nx.read_pajek("LiveJournalData.net") function can be used.

4.8 Social Network Analysis

Social network analysis is involved in the analysis of the structure of relations among actors (people, groups of people, or organizations, among many others). It is an approach in social research with four distinctive characteristics: systematic relational data, structural intuition, graphical models, and mathematical models. By looking at life as consisting of relations and the patterns that are formed from these relations, SNA starts its methodology. It is a science in which people influence each other in a way that leads to the construction of knowledge body (Freeman 2004, p. 6).

The ultimate goal of SNA is to examine the relations between individuals within a social network, which can have the meaning of influence, affection, communication, advice, friendship, trust, dislike, conflict, or many other things, in addition to the overall network structure. Hence, researchers are interested in studying such relations and their influence on both individual behavior and group performance.

It is involved in the investigation of individual's behavior (e.g., a person or organization) at three levels of analysis, micro, meso, and macro, in addition to the interactions between them. Therefore, network analysts are either involved in the analysis of a network as a whole (sociocentric analysis), a part of the network (subnetwork analysis), or the connections of one specific node (ego-network analysis).

Evolving from solely a proposed metaphor to an analytic tool, and finally to a scientific paradigm, SNA today has its concepts, methods, applications, analytic software, as well as professional researchers. It received lots of interest from researchers in computer science, economics, anthropology, biology, etc., where it has become a powerful analytic tool for many real-world implementations.

The way that social network analysts collect and analyze data is different from what social scientists are used to Marin and Wellman.

However, SNA suffers from some issues related to trust, privacy, and strategy in organizations and shortage of providing successful results for certain implementations such as in education evaluation.

4.9   Social Network Analysis vs. Link Analysis

Another concept that is similar in many ways to SNA is link analysis. They share the same idea of using nodes and edges to model networks, and both try to find the key players in a network. However, link analysis allows for different types of nodes and edges to coexist on the same network which may produce invalid results. The way that SNA uses to solve the problem of having a network with different types of nodes and edges is by using multimode networks.

4.10   Historical Development

Social network analysis emerged as a result of cooperation between three different disciplines: (1) sociometric analysts who came up with technical advancements in graph theory by working with small groups of data, (2) Harvard researchers who in 1930s discovered patterns of interpersonal relations and the formation of cliques, and (3) Manchester anthropologists who studied people connections and community structures in tribal and village societies.

The roots of SNA go back as far as 1934 when Jacob Moreno wrote his popular book "who shall survive?" which was a turning point in the development of the field, added to later significant contributions in social network theory and research introduced by a group of researchers at Harvard University in the 1970s.

Alfred Radcliffe-Brown, one of the famous English social anthropologists, also participated in a nontechnical fashion in the development of SNA through his studies on structural functionalism and coadaptation, while the period from the 1930s to the 1970s witnessed an increasing number of researchers, who built on Alfred's concepts in the social structure.

In addition to Moreno and Radcliffe-Brown, some other scientists also contributed to the expansion of the field using systematic methods including Stephen Borgatti, Kathleen Carely, Linton Freeman, Stanley Wasserman, and Harrison White.

Four features characterize the current use of SNA:

- The study of SNA is motivated by the structural composition of ties that link social actors.
- SNA is built on systematic empirical inputs.
- SNA relies heavily on the use of graphical representations.
- SNA also relies on the use of computational and mathematical models.

SNA is not only defined by these four attributes, but rather, it goes beyond to extend a variety of growing applications (Freeman 2004, pp. 3–5). Nevertheless, only recently were the four constituents combined into an integral scientific research model as social analysts were used to implementing one or some of them at one time.

As soon as the social network community found that SNA structural approach could be generalized, some useful applications for different experimental environments became available.

A study was conducted by Otte and Rousseau in 2002 to measure the growth of SNA field during the period from 1963 to 2000. They consulted three databases that related to three areas in science (i.e., sociology, medicine, and psychology) while considering only the studies that have "social network analysis" in the "subject heading" field. A total number of 1601 articles in sociology, 308 articles and psychology in medicine, and 105 articles in psychology were retrieved. The study shows that the real growth of the field began in 1981 with no signs of decline followed that. It also indicates that the development in the field began first in sociology followed by medicine and then psychology. The success that social network analysis achieved in the eighties of the last century was a result to SNA institutionalization in the late seventies added to some textbooks and computer software being published.

Today, SN analysts have their international organization known as "International Network for Social Network Analysis" or INSNA that organizes annual meetings and issues professional publications. Also, some centers for network research have opened worldwide, and a growing number of general and technical courses are offered by universities.

4.11 Importance of Social Network Analysis

Scientists of social network analysis analyze network data at different levels, starting from individuals, families, and groups, up to the level of nations. Thus, they perform a critical job determining how to solve issues in society, how organizations can be better run, and how individuals can achieve their goals faster. Though relatively new, social network analysis has become, alongside statistics, a powerful methodological tool across different disciplines. In descriptive SNA applications, the implementation involves the analysis of the structural aspects of the network, while in explanative SNA applications, the implementation is concerned with explaining how node attributes are dependent on their structural embedding within the network.

The use of SNA was received with applause by scientists and researchers from different scientific fields when they realized its importance as a potentially successful analysis tool for many implementations. For instance, SNA was successfully applied in (1) health, in research related to the epidemiology and prevention of sexually transmitted diseases; (2) cybercrime, investigating online hacker communities; (3) business, studying the influence of SNA and sentiment analysis in predicting business trends; (4) animal social networks, investigating the relationships and the social structures of animal gatherings and the direct and indirect interactions between groups; and (5) communications, studying the different structural properties of short message service graphs. Additionally, SNA has been in other places, alongside other tools, such as in information retrieval, information fusion communities, and investigation of terrorist groups.

4.12 Social Network Analysis Modeling Tools

Social network analysis modeling tools are software packages that can be used to identify, represent, analyze, and visualize social networks. Examples include Pajek: software for analysis and visualization of large networks, UCINET, StOCENT, Gephi, Network Workbench, and NodeXL.

Special-purposes SNA modeling tools can be used to carry out particular analysis tasks such as the identification of subgroups, knowledge networks, hidden populations, kinship networks, and structural networks. Examples include NEGOPY, InFlow, and SocioMetric LinkAlyzer. Some modeling tools have programming utility such as NetworkX, JUNG, iGraph, Prefuse, and SNAP.

Because most of the concepts and techniques that social network analysis is based on are taken from mathematical graph theory, it is indispensable to spend some time briefing the main concepts in graph theory.

The main goal of SNA is to find local and global patterns, identify influential actors, and investigate network dynamics. Therefore, SNA is involved in the analysis of ties between people, organizations, and even countries.

Throughout the following three chapters, we will go through three levels of analyses including finding key players in the social network at the ego (individual) level, detecting distinctive communities in networks at the group level, and finally implementing cohesion analyses at the network level.

References

Borgatti SP, Foster PC (2003) The network paradigm in organizational research: a review and typology. J Manag 29(6):991–1013

Freeman LC (2004) The development of social network analysis: a study in the sociology of science. BookSurge, LLC, North Charleston

Marin A, Wellman B (2010) Social network analysis: an introduction. In: Carrington P, Scott J (eds) Handbook of social network analysis. SAGE Publications, London

Wasserman S, Faust K (1994) Social network analysis: methods and applications. Cambridge University Press, Cambridge

Chapter 5
Node-Level Analysis

This chapter is concerned with building an understanding of how to do network analysis at the node (ego) level. It shows how to create social networks from scratch, how to import networks, how to find key players in social networks using centrality measures, and how to visualize networks. We will also introduce the important algorithms that are used to gain insights from graphs.

5.1 Ego-Network Analysis

The ego-centered network is a network commonly seen from a particular actor at its center. By changing the actor of interest (the focal actor or ego), we can navigate different regions of the entire network. In these networks, the focal actor is the center of the analysis, rather than the entire set of actors.

Ego-centered network analysis has its roots in both the social support literature and in the literature that uses large-scale survey studies to understand people's relationships. All the information on the network comes from the focal actor, which means that it is not important to know whether alters do exist nor whether they are connected to each other. The ego-centered paradigm has received great interest in the 2000s with the advent of popular social networking sites such as Facebook and LinkedIn.

Ego-network analysis involves the examination of the relations that extend from a particular individual (or sample of individuals) outward to their contacts. Ego-centered network type of analysis can be utilized, for example, to collect information on the relationships within a certain setting, such as a classroom in a school or a department in a corporation.

During their work, network analysts may diverge their attention from studying the characteristics of the entire network (which is called sociocentric analysis) toward examining the subnetwork of one particular node (which is called egocentric network analysis). Both the so-called ego-centered network and complete

© Springer International Publishing AG 2017

M.Z. Al-Taie, S. Kadry, *Python for Graph and Network Analysis*, Advanced Information and Knowledge Processing, DOI 10.1007/978-3-319-53004-8_5

network analyses are the two strands of research networks. Both of them developed relatively independent of each other and do not take much not of each other. While complete network data analysis largely focuses on structural properties like density, betweenness, and clusters/cliques, ego-centered data analysis focuses more on the content of the relationship of an actor such as with whom one discusses personal matters, when as where has met, and multiplexity of the relationship, which means how many layers that relationship has. It should be noted that the two approaches of network analysis do not compete but rather complete each other. Typically we look at both the composition of the ego network and the complete network structure (e.g., density and number of components).

The size of the ego network can be understood from the number of alters (an actor or another entity with a relation with ego) that the network has. Those alters form what is called a "component" in which they have cohesive relations among them and weak relations to the other actors. The relations between the ego and the alters in the component are a string which means the density of ego's relations with the alters in this component is high. The alters of one component are characterized by being interrelated, sharing an attribute, having a joint affiliation, or occurring together. Understanding the structure of a component will help in understanding and analyzing the environment around the ego. There could be more than one component attached to the ego network where each component has its size and its density. Even though ego can relate to many components (a network property called "diversity"), ego's relations are concentered on a few number of these components, leaving the other component without prominence (a network property called hierarchy or stratification).

For the purpose of analysis, each of these two trends has its type of software. For example, UCINET is a program of choice for complete network analysis, while SPSS and STATA can be both used for ego-centered networks.

Collecting data on a network is typically interesting when the population of a network is too large. In this case, we select a sample of objects (egos) and collect data about them and also about their neighbors (alters) and links among them (Fig. 5.1).

The ego-centric analysis is a very useful way to understand complicated network structures and to see how they arise from the local connections of individual actors. By collecting information on the subnetwork that is centered on a certain node (such a subnetwork is called ego network), we can build a picture of the local networks of that node (or individual). Friendship connections on Facebook or LinkedIn websites are examples of subnetworks that are centered on a certain node which is, in this case, the account holder.

Example 1

In this example, we are going to create a NetworkX object of the Davis Southern Women graph, draw the histogram and then draw the graph using matplotlib package:

```
In:    g = nx.davis_southern_women_graph()
```

Fig. 5.1 Ego network of one focal node (maximized here) and nine alters

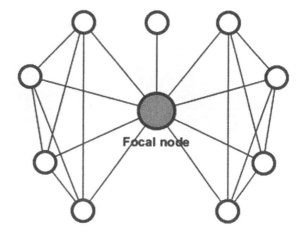

Let's check the list of nodes and edges of the graph:

```
In:    g.nodes()
Out:
       ['Flora Price', 'Nora Fayette', 'E10', 'Verne Sanderson', 'E12',
       'E14', Frances Anderson', 'Dorothy Murchison', 'Evelyn Jefferson',
       'Ruth DeSand', Helen Lloyd', 'Olivia Carleton', 'Eleanor Nye',
       'E11', 'E9', 'E8', 'E5', E4', 'E7', 'E6', 'E1', 'Myra Liddel',
       'E3', 'E2', 'Theresa Anderson', Pearl glethorpe', 'Katherina
       Rogers', 'Brenda Rogers', 'E13', 'Charlotte McDowd', Sylvia
       Avondale', 'Laura Mandeville']
```

An important measure of a node in a graph is degree which, for undirected graphs, is the number of connections the node has. For directed graphs, on the other hand, a node may have two types of degree. The in-degree represents the inbound links of the node, while the out-degree represents the outbound links of the node. Let's calculate the degree of every node of this graph:

To visualize the figure:

```
In:  plt.figure(figsize=(10, 10))
     pos = nx.random_layout(g)
     nx.draw(g, node_size = 90, node_color='cyan', with_labels=False)
     nx.draw_networkx_labels(g, pos)
     plt.show()
```

We get the following graph (Fig. 5.2):

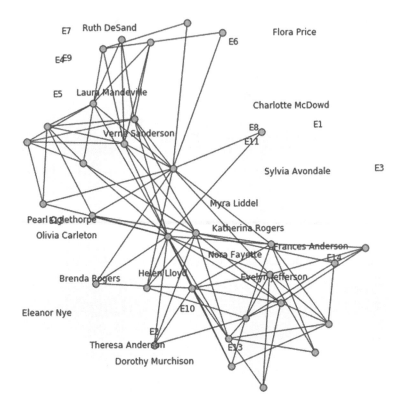

Fig. 5.2 Davis Southern Women graph

```
In:    g.degree()
Out:
       {'Brenda Rogers': 7, 'Charlotte McDowd': 4, 'Dorothy Murchison': 2,
       'E1': , 'E10': 5, 'E11': 4, 'E12': 6, 'E13': 3, 'E14': 3, 'E2': 3,
       'E3': 6, 'E4': , 'E5': 8, 'E6': 8, 'E7': 10, 'E8': 14, 'E9': 12,
       'Eleanor Nye': 4, 'Evelyn efferson': 8, 'Flora Price': 2, 'Frances
       Anderson': 4, 'Helen Lloyd': 5, Katherina Rogers': 6, 'Laura
       Mandeville': 7, 'Myra Liddel': 4, 'Nora ayette': 8, 'Olivia
       Carleton': 2, 'Pearl Oglethorpe': 3, 'Ruth DeSand': 4, Sylvia
       Avondale': 7, 'Theresa Anderson': 8, 'Verne Sanderson': 4}
```

It is common for graphs (especially for large graphs) to use a histogram to
approximate the degree distribution of nodes. Let's suppose that we have a random
graph with 5000 nodes and the link probability is 0.01. The histogram of the node
degree will be as follows (Fig. 5.3):

Fig. 5.3 Degree
distribution of a random
graph with 5000 nodes

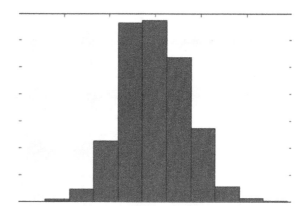

```
In:   plt.hist(nx.fast_gnp_random_graph(5000, 0.01).degree().values())
Out:  (array([   13.,      94.,     451.,   1330.,   1345.,   1074.,    547.,
      114.,              26.,       6.]), array([ 26. ,   31.3,  36.6,   41.9,
      47.2,   52.5,   57.8,   63.1,   68.4, 73.7,   79. ]),
      <a list of 10 Patch objects>)
```

Returning to our example, let's draw the histogram of the Davis Southern Women
graph (Fig. 5.4):

```
In:   plt.figure(1)
      plt.hist(nx.degree(g).values())
Out:

      (array([ 8.,   8.,   2.,   3.,   3.,   5.,   1.,   0.,   1.,   1.]),
       array([ 2. ,    3.2,    4.4,    5.6,    6.8,    8. ,    9.2,   10.4,
      11.6, 12.8,   14. ]),
       <a list of 10 Patch objects>)
```

Now, let's extract an ego network from the Davis Southern Women graph.
NetworkX provides a ready-made function to do the extraction. The function will
return a graph object that we can implement all network operations on (Fig. 5.5):

```
In:   nx.ego_graph(g, 'Theresa Anderson')
Out:  <networkx.classes.graph.Graph at 0xd735b00>

In:   ego_net = nx.ego_graph(g, 'Theresa Anderson')

In:   print(nx.info(ego_net))
Out:  Name:
      Type: Graph
      Number of nodes: 9
      Number of edges: 8
      Average degree:   1.7778
In:   pos=nx.shell_layout(ego_net)
      nx.draw_networkx(ego_net, pos, node_size=800, node_color='magenta')

Out:
```

Fig. 5.4 Degree
distribution of the Davis
Southern Women network

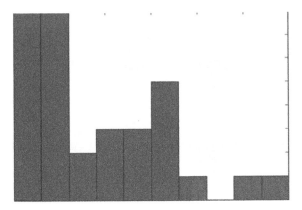

Fig. 5.5 Ego network of
one node from the Davis
Southern Women graph

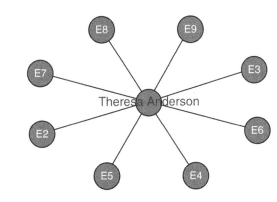

Fig. 5.6 Barabasi-Albert
graph with 1000 nodes

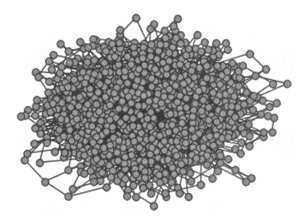

Example 2

In this example, we are going first to build a graph based on the Barabasi-Albert
model with n = 1000 nodes and m = 2 min degree for each node. After that, we are
going to extract a subgraph from the original graph to represent the network of the
node with the largest degree in the network (Figs. 5.6 and 5.7).

Fig. 5.7 Ego network of a
node from Barabasi-Albert
graph

```
# Create a Barabasi-Albert graph model
In:  G = nx.barabasi_albert_graph(1000, 2)


# Let's draw the graph
In:  pos= nx.spring_layout(G)
In:  nx.draw(G, pos, node_color='c', node_size=60 ,with_labels=False)


# find node with largest degree
In:    node_degree = G.degree()

# calculate number of nodes
In:    G.order()
Ou:    1000


# calculate number of edges
In:    G.size()
Out:   1996

# find node with the largest degree
In:    node_degree= G.degree()
In:    (largest_deg, degree)=
sorted(node_degree.items(),key=itemgetter(1))[-1]

# Create ego graph of node with the largest degree
In:    node_ego= nx.ego_graph(G,largest_deg)

# Draw ego graph
In:    pos= nx.spring_layout(node_ego)
In:    nx.draw(node_ego, pos, node_color='c', node_size=120
,with_labels=False)
```

Example 3

In this example, we will discover the Marvel Universe Social Graph dataset introduced by Cesc Rosselló, Ricardo Alberich, and Joe Miro. The dataset was created by compiling characters with the comic book in which they appear. The dataset has the csv format, weighs around 21 MB, and has 6426 nodes and 167,219 edges. Let's first import the important libraries for this example:

```
In:    import networkx as nx
       import unicodecsv as csv
       import numpy as np
       import scipy.stats
       import matplotlib.pyplot as plt
       from operator import itemgetter
```

Next, let's define a function that is going to build our "Heroic Network" by adding edges between heroes (hence, nodes are added automatically) based on the dataset that we pass to the function (hero-to-hero) network:

```
In:    def graph_func(path):
            graph = nx.Graph(name="Heroic Network")
            with open(path, 'rU') as data:
                reader = csv.reader(data)
                for row in reader:
                    graph.add_edge(*row)
            return graph
```

We will call the function and pass the relative path of the dataset (hero-network.csv). The result of invoking the function is assigned to a new variable called graph:

```
graph = graph_func("dataset_local_path")
```

Next, we compute number of nodes and number of edges:

```
In:    graph.order()
Out:   6426
In:    graph.size()
Out:   167219
```

```
In:    graph.nodes()
Out:
       [u'QUESADA, JOE', u'ZEITGEIST II/AXEL CL', u'LOGA II',
       u'PIECEMEAL/GILBERT E', u'BENWAY, DR.', u'FRIEDLANDER, SHARON',
       u'DREAMING CELESTIAL/T', 'MODRED THE MYSTIC', u'THOMAS, DR. STAN',
       u'FIREWALL/THEARY/MIN ', u'DR. AUSTUS', u'RAYMOND, NORA JONES',
       u'DEATHRAVEN/JOSHUA RA', u'MARROW/SARAH ', u'EPOCH',……….]
```

Let's take a look at a snapshot from the edges that are present in the network, which represent the hero-to-hero connections that imply the "knows" relationship:

```
In:      graph.edges()
Out:
         [(u'QUESADA, JOE', u'ZURI'),
          (u'QUESADA, JOE', u'GLADIATOR/MELVIN POT'),
          (u'QUESADA, JOE', u'SMITH, KEVIN'),
          (u'QUESADA, JOE', u'OKOYE'),
          (u'QUESADA, JOE', u'RALF'),
          (u'QUESADA, JOE', u'PALMIOTTI, JIMMY'),
          (u'QUESADA, JOE', u'BLAKE, BECKY'),
          (u'QUESADA, JOE', u'MYSTERIO/QUENTIN BEC'),
          (u'QUESADA, JOE', u'WATSON-PARKER, MARY '),
          (u'QUESADA, JOE', u'QUINN, ASHLEY'),
          (u'QUESADA, JOE', u'MCKENZIE, LYDIA'),......]
```

This network is too big to visualize using NetworkX library only. Rather, let's calculate some overall information for the "Heroic Network" using the built-in nx. info() method from NetworkX library:

```
In:    nx.info(graph)
Out:
       'Name: Heroic Social Network\nType: Graph\nNumber of nodes:
       6426\nNumber of edges: 167219\nAverage degree: 52.0445'
```

We are going to extract a smaller network from the previous Heroic Network (hero-to-hero network). The new derived network is going to include the comic book in which each character appears, which means building a "hero-to-comic" network that represents the source of their relationship.

By computing the comics that heroes appear in together, we can compute the strength of the "knows" relationships in the way that the more two heroes appear in together in a comic, the better they probably know each other.

The following code is extracted from the book:

```
def graph_from_gdf(path):
    graph = nx.Graph(name="Characters in Comics")
    with open(path, 'rU') as data:
        reader = csv.reader(data)
        for row in reader:
            if 'nodedef' in row[0]:
                handler = lambda row,G: G.add_node(row[0],
TYPE=row[1])
            elif 'edgedef' in row[0]:
                handler = lambda row,G: G.add_edge(*row)
            else:
                handler(row, graph)
    return graph
```

We will call the function and pass the relative path of the dataset (comic-hero-network.gdf).

```
graph = graph_from_gdf("dataset_local_path")

In:    nx.info(graph)
       Out:    'Name: Characters in Comics\nType: Graph\nNumber of nodes:
       19090\nNumber of edges: 96104\nAverage degree:  10.0685'

In:    graph.order()
Out:   19090

In:    graph.size()
Out:   96104
```

Now, we are going to extract a subgraph for a particular node (hero) from the comic-to-hero network. The goal is to get a feel of what is happening in the network at the ego (individual) level.

Extracting an ego graph from a bigger network has a straightforward implementation in NetworkX. The function takes three arguments: the expanded social graph, the ego node, and the maximum path length.

```
ego_net = nx.ego_graph(graph, character, hops)
```

Defining the ego network is relational and is bound by how many hops (n-step neighborhood) we want to jump after we leave the ego node.

```
In:    graph = graph_from_gdf(".../comic-hero-network.gdf")

In:    graph.order()
Out:   19090

In:    graph.size()
Out:   96104
```

Suppose that we want to study "GRIFFIN II/JOHNNY HO" ego network and that we want to consider at first only the direct neighbors (also called alters) of that hero. The number of hops, in this case, is one (Fig. 5.8).

```
In:    ego_net = nx.ego_graph(graph, "GRIFFIN II/JOHNNY HO", 1)
```

Now, let's plot the ego network:

```
In: plt.figure(figsize=(10, 10))
    pos = nx.spring_layout(ego_net)
    nx.draw_networkx(ego_net, pos, with_labels=True, node_size=800,
    alpha=1, node_color='r')
```

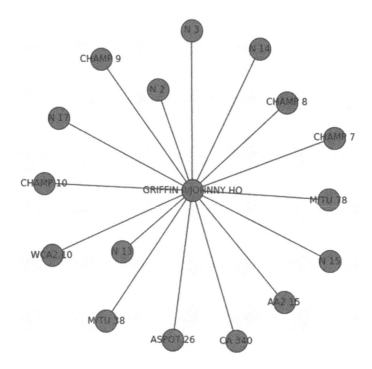

Fig. 5.8 Ego network of a node from the Marvel Universe graph

The preceding one-hop graph shows the hero Johnny Ho (also known as Griffin II) situated at the center of the graph and connected to the comics where he appears. It looks that he appears in 16 places (AA2 15, ASPOT 26, CA 340, and so on). This can also be confirmed if we calculate number of nodes and number of edges:

```
In:     ego_net.order()
Out:    17

In:     ego_net.size()
Out:    16
```

Alternatively, if we want to consider two hops rather than one hop (meaning that we are taking in the neighbors of the ego's direct neighbors) (Fig. 5.9):

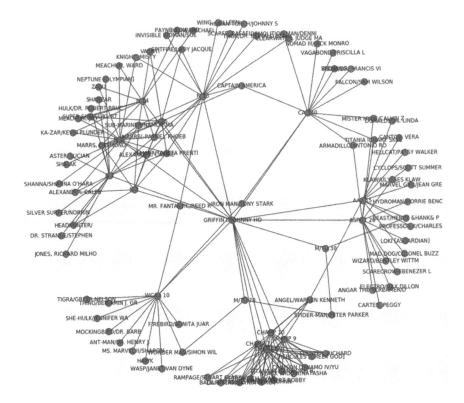

Fig. 5.9 Ego network of a node with two hops

```
In:     ego_net = nx.ego_graph(graph, "GRIFFIN II/JOHNNY HO", 2)

In:     ego_net.order()
Out:    100

In:     ego_net.size()
Out:    175

In:     plt.figure(figsize=(20, 20))
        pos = nx.spring_layout(ego_net)
        nx.draw_networkx(ego_net, pos, with_labels=True, node_size=800,
        alpha=1, node_color='r')
```

The above two-hop graph expands the volume of the network by including the neighbors of the direct neighbors. The ego Griffin II is still present at the center of the graph.

Now, let's also try three hops(Fig. 5.10):

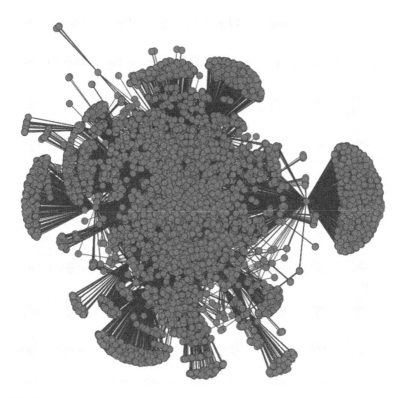

Fig. 5.10 Ego network of a node with three hops

```
In:    ego_net = nx.ego_graph(graph, "GRIFFIN II/JOHNNY HO", 3)

In:    ego_net.order()
Out:   8163

In:    ego_net.order()
Out:   20797


In:    plt.figure(figsize=(20, 20))
       pos = nx.spring_layout(ego_net)
       nx.draw_networkx(ego_net, pos, with_labels=True, node_size=200,
       alpha=1, node_color='r')
```

The above three-hop graph considerably expands the size of the network. It considers three hops. Clusters are readily apparent, although ego network is no more to be seen.

5.2   Identifying Influential Individuals in the Network

In all types of networks, nodes are usually not independent of each other. Rather, they are connected by one or more ties. Since these nodes are connected, they could influence each other. One question arises here: which nodes, among a large number of connected nodes, are more important?

Centrality measures can answer such a question. They have the ability to capture the importance of nodes in different perspectives.

A centrality measure is an important graph analytic that gives insight into the relative importance of a particular node in a graph (or persons in a network). The individuals who work in less constrained environments and have more chances than others are in favorable structural positions. Having a favorable position means that the individual can practice better bargains in exchanges, have a greater effect, and become focal of other persons in less favored positions regarding deference and attention. The importance of identifying key players in a network is that it shows how active each user is since active actors are more likely to establish social ties with a large number of actors in the network.

Centrality is a term used to define the importance of a node. Centrality is one of the most used measures to find out how central a person is in a network (which may be a social club or the World Wide Web). The most commonly used measures are degree, closeness, betweenness, and eigenvector centralities. Although they are important, centrality measures alone are usually not enough to analyze a social network in the way that finding the most influential persons (key users) in a network requires the analysis of the network structure.

Centrality measures and network structure can both be used to understand the structure and organization of malicious networks and to locate suspicious nodes in these networks. This has the benefit of destabilizing and reducing the effectiveness of the underlying social network.

To find the important players in a network, some measures were developed for this purpose including eigenvector, degree, closeness, and betweenness centralities. Previous research has shown that the three measures are highly correlated and give similar results in the identification of most important actors in a network. Most of the time, three out of four or all the four centrality metrics will land a person (or persons) in the top ten of any centrality list.

In this section, we will cover the four standard centrality measures of power and influence and discuss their implementation over several datasets.

5.2.1   Degree Centrality

Degree centrality considers the node with the highest degree (largest number of connections) as the most central node in the network. Degree centrality focuses on individual nodes—it simply counts the number of edges that a node has.

Fig. 5.11 Krackhardt kite
graph

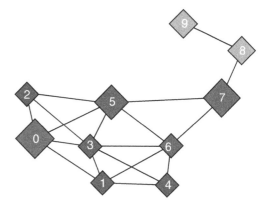

Degree centrality is a measure of popularity that determines the nodes that can quickly spread information to a localized area. On Facebook, it is simply the number of friends. On Twitter, it is the number of followers, and on a site like Reddit, it is the number of upvotes.

Example 1

In the next example, we will analyze the Krackhardt Kite graph. This kite-like graph has been studied well in the social network literature to show the differences between the different network centrality measures. The edges are not directed as they imply mutual acceptance criteria.

The graph consists of ten nodes and has the shape of a kite. It consists of two different groups of nodes. The first group has from zero to six of interlinked nodes, whereas the second group has from seven to nine of a chain-like shape of nodes (Fig. 5.11).

```
import networkx as nx
%matplotlib inline
import matplotlib.pyplot as plt

In:   g = nx.krackhardt_kite_graph()

In:   colors = ['r', 'g', 'g', 'g', 'g', 'm', 'm', 'r', 'c', 'c']
      sizes =  [800, 300, 300, 300, 300, 600, 300, 800, 400, 400]
      labels = {0: '0', 1:'1', 2:'2', 3:'3', 4:'4', 5:'5', 6:'6', 7:'7',
      8:'8', 9:'9'}

In:   nx.draw_networkx(g, node_color=colors,
      node_shape='D',with_labels=True, labels=labels,node_size=sizes)
      plt.show()
```

One observation from the figure above is that the Krackhardt Kite graph consists of a single big core and a small periphery.

Python NetworkX library provides a straightforward method to calculate degree centrality. It returns degree as a Python map, which is a set of node-value pairs linking node number (or node name, in other cases) to the degree value:

```
In: nx.degree_centrality(g)
Out: {0: 0.4444444444444444,
    1: 0.4444444444444444,
    2: 0.3333333333333333,
    3: 0.6666666666666666,
    4: 0.3333333333333333,
    5: 0.5555555555555556,
    6: 0.5555555555555556,
    7: 0.3333333333333333,
    8: 0.2222222222222222,
    9: 0.1111111111111111}
```

Let's rearrange the result from highest to lowest degree centrality:

```
In:   print(sorted(nx.degree_centrality(g).items(),key=itemgetter(1),
      reverse=True))
Out:
[(3, 0.6666666666666666), (5, 0.5555555555555556), (6, 0.5555555555555556),
(0, 0.4444444444444444), (1, 0.4444444444444444), (2, 0.3333333333333333),
(4, 0.3333333333333333), (7, 0.3333333333333333), (8, 0.2222222222222222),
(9, 0.1111111111111111)]
```

Note that node 3 achieves the highest level of degree centrality since it has the maximum number of connections (6). On the other hand, node 9 has the lowest degree since it is connected to only one other node.

As you can see, the range between the minimum and maximum degree is significant. Let's check the degree distribution (Fig. 5.12):

```
In:   degree = nx.degree(g)
      plt.hist(degree.values(), bins = 10)
      plt.title("Degree Values for the Krackhardt Kite Graph")
      plt.xlabel("Degree")
      plt.ylabel("Frequency")
      plt.show()
Out:
```

The figure above shows the distribution of degrees of the Krackhardt Kite graph. A larger number of nodes have a distribution that is located near the mean, while a

Fig. 5.12 Degree
distribution of the nodes in
the Krackhardt Kite graph

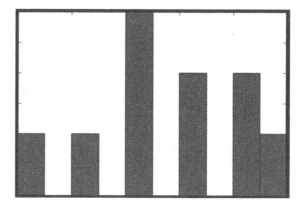

small number of nodes have a distribution located at both sides of the mean. This
gives the impression that the current distribution is somehow similar to the normal
distribution, which is symmetric and has bell-shaped curves with a single peak.

Example 2

Continuing our work on the hero social network, we will see who the key players
are in the network of comic book characters.

Let's start by computing the node degree of each hero in the hero-to-hero network and choose only the top ten nodes:

```
In:      import operator
In:      graph = graph_from_csv("…/hero-network.csv")
In:      all_deg = sorted(graph.degree().items(),
key=operator.itemgetter(1), reverse=True)

In:      for node in all_deg[0:10]: print node
Out:
         (u'CAPTAIN AMERICA', 1908)
         (u'SPIDER-MAN/PETER PAR', 1737)
         (u'IRON MAN/TONY STARK ', 1522)
         (u'THING/BENJAMIN J. GR', 1416)
         (u'MR. FANTASTIC/REED R', 1379)
         (u'WOLVERINE/LOGAN ', 1371)
         (u'HUMAN TORCH/JOHNNY S', 1361)
         (u'SCARLET WITCH/WANDA ', 1325)
         (u'THOR/DR. DONALD BLAK', 1289)
         (u'BEAST/HENRY &HANK& P', 1267)
```

Another way to calculate the top ten heroes in the hero-to-hero network is by
using a helpful function, degree_centrality, from NetworkX, which allows us to
compute the percent of nodes that each node is connected to.

```
In:      centrality = nx.degree_centrality(graph)
In:      all_deg = sorted(centrality.items(), key=itemgetter(1),
reverse=True)

In:      for node in all_deg[0:10:]: print "%s: %0.3f" % node
Out:
         CAPTAIN AMERICA: 0.297
         SPIDER-MAN/PETER PAR: 0.270
         IRON MAN/TONY STARK : 0.237
         THING/BENJAMIN J. GR: 0.220
         MR. FANTASTIC/REED R: 0.215
         WOLVERINE/LOGAN : 0.213
         HUMAN TORCH/JOHNNY S: 0.212
         SCARLET WITCH/WANDA : 0.206
         THOR/DR. DONALD BLAK: 0.201
         BEAST/HENRY &HANK& P: 0.197
```

We might like to calculate the average degree of the hero-to-hero network. To do this, we need to find the degree of each node, sum them up together, and then divide the result by the total number of nodes in the network:

```
In:      degrees = graph.degree()
         sum_of_edges = sum(degrees.values())

In:      avg_deg = float(sum_of_edges/(graph.order()))
         print(avg_deg)
Out:     52.0
```

A better way to represent node degrees is by using a histogram. NetworkX has a function called degree_histogram. However, this function returns a long list of the frequencies of the degrees, which may not be informative enough for us.

```
In:    nx.degree_histogram(graph)
Out:
       [0, 53, 86, 104, 150, 182, 178, 185, 230, 224, 245, 254, 187, 194,
       60, 193, 123, 143, 123, 108, 131, 119,…]
```

A better way would be by using the matplotlib library from Python and particularly the plt.hist() function as follows (Fig. 5.13):

```
In:      plt.hist(graph.degree().values(), bins=500)
         plt.title("Degree Values of the Hero Network")
         plt.xlabel("Degree")
         plt.ylabel("Frequency")
         plt.show()

Out:
```

Fig. 5.13 Degree
distribution of the
hero-to-hero network

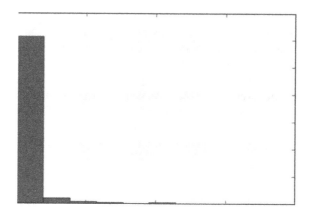

5.2.2   Closeness Centrality

To determine the central nodes in networks, the closeness centrality measure considers the nodes that have the smallest average path length (sequence of relationships) for the nodes that are linked to other nodes. Closeness centrality is important because it takes into account not only the immediate connections of an actor (this is what degree centrality measure does) but also the indirect ties of all other nodes in the network. It is a measure of reach, how fast information will spread to all other nodes from a single node.

Example 1
Following up with our Krackhardt Kite graph example, the following code can be used to calculate the closeness centrality for all the nodes in the example graph:

```
In:   nx.closeness_centrality(g)
Out: {0: 0.5294117647058824,
 1: 0.5294117647058824,
 2: 0.5,
 3: 0.6,
 4: 0.5,
 5: 0.6428571428571429,
 6: 0.6428571428571429,
 7: 0.6,
 8: 0.42857142857142855,
 9: 0.3103448275862069}

In:   print(sorted(nx.closeness_centrality(g).items(),key=itemgetter(1),
      reverse=True))
Out:
      [(5, 0.6428571428571429), (6, 0.6428571428571429), (3, 0.6), (7,
      0.6), (0, 0.5294117647058824), (1, 0.5294117647058824), (2, 0.5),
      (4, 0.5), (8, 0.42857142857142855), (9, 0.3103448275862069)]
```

As you can imagine, nodes 3, 5, and 6 achieve the highest closeness centrality degrees since they are present in the middle of the network and can reach other nodes with a few number of steps. However, why do these nodes have such high closeness centrality? It is due to their structural positions. They are located in the core of the Krackhardt Kite graph where they have more connections and hence shorter average distance. We can compare this to a node like 9 which is located in the periphery at the far end of the Krackhardt Kite graph. It achieves the lowest of both degree and closeness centralities.

Let's look at the distribution of closeness centrality of the Krackhardt Kite.

```
In:   closeness = nx.closeness(g)
      plt.hist(closeness.values(), bins = 10)
      plt.title("Closeness Values for the Krackhardt Kite Graph")
      plt.xlabel("Closeness")
      plt.ylabel("Frequency")
      plt.show()
Out:
```

As the distribution of closeness centrality shows, the closeness centrality is not so heavily skewed. Only a few nodes are still forming the graph tail, whereas the rest of nodes align to a bell curve at the low end of the spectrum. This shows that the core of the graph consists of nodes that are no more than two steps away from each other.

Example 2
We can also check the closeness centrality for the hero-to-hero graph and find the ten heroes that have the top closeness centralities. We are going to calculate this value in three different tastes: without arguments, normalized for the number of nodes in the graph, or weighted to incorporate edge weights:

```
In:   close_cent = nx.betweenness_centrality(graph)
      norm_close_cent = nx.betweenness_centrality(graph, normalized=True)
      weigh_close_cent = nx.betweenness_centrality(graph,
weight="weight")
```

The method that is faster than the two other methods is the normalized one. Hence, we are going to use its result when we calculate the top ten nodes:

```
In:    all_close = sorted(norm_close_cent.items(), key=itemgetter(1),
reverse=True)
```

```
In:    for node in all_close[0:10:]: print "%s: %0.3f" % node
Out:
```

```
       SPIDER-MAN/PETER PAR: 0.074
       CAPTAIN AMERICA: 0.057
       IRON MAN/TONY STARK : 0.037
       WOLVERINE/LOGAN : 0.036
       HAVOK/ALEX SUMMERS : 0.036
       DR. STRANGE/STEPHEN : 0.029
       THING/BENJAMIN J. GR: 0.025
       HAWK: 0.025
       HULK/DR. ROBERT BRUC: 0.024
       MR. FANTASTIC/REED R: 0.024
```

As we can see in the above list of heroes, it is identical to the list that we got when we implemented the degree centrality measure.

5.2.3 Betweenness Centrality

While degree and closeness centralities are based on the concept of the person's reachability, betweenness centrality, on the other hand, relies on the idea that a person is more important if he/she is more intermediary in the network. This measure is based on the notion of geodesics, which means that an actor can become more important in the network if he/she is situated on the geodesics between many pairs of actors in the network. Nodes that occur on many shortest paths between other nodes in the graph have a high betweenness centrality score.

Example 1
To implement the betweenness centrality measure for the Krackhardt Kite graph, a straightforward way in NetworkX can look like this:

```
In:   nx.betweenness_centrality(g)
      Out: {0: 0.023148148148148143,

      1: 0.023148148148148143,
      2: 0.0,
      3: 0.10185185185185183,
      4: 0.0,
      5: 0.23148148148148148,
      6: 0.23148148148148148,
      7: 0.38888888888888884,
      8: 0.2222222222222222,
      9: 0.0}

In:  print(sorted(nx.betweenness_centrality(g).items(),key=itemgetter(1),
       reverse=True))

Out:

      [(7, 0.38888888888888884), (5, 0.23148148148148148), (6,
      0.23148148148148148), (8, 0.2222222222222222), (3,
      0.10185185185185183), (0, 0.023148148148148143), (1,
      0.023148148148148143), (2, 0.0), (4, 0.0), (9, 0.0)]
```

As you can see, node 7 achieves the highest betweenness centrality degree. This is evident since it is the only node that connects the nodes in the periphery (8 and 9) to the nodes in the core. On the other extreme, nodes 9 and 8 are located at the border of the network and are not present in any of the shortest paths of the network.

Example 2

We can also check the betweenness centrality for the hero-to-hero graph and find the ten heroes that have the top betweenness centralities. We are going to calculate this value in three different cases: without arguments, normalized for the number of nodes in the graph, or weighted to incorporate edge weights:

```
In:   bet_cent = nx.betweenness_centrality(graph)
      norm_bet_cent = nx.betweenness_centrality(graph, normalized=True)
      weigh_bet_cent = nx.betweenness_centrality(graph, weight="weight")

Out:
```

As we did when we calculated degree centrality for the top ten nodes in the network, we are going to calculate between centrality for the top nodes in the same network (using the normalized version of the function) and see if they give us the same results as before!

```
In:     all_bet = sorted(norm_bet_cent.items(), key=itemgetter(1),
reverse=True)

In:     for node in all_bet[0:10:]: print "%s: %0.3f" % node
Out:
        SPIDER-MAN/PETER PAR: 0.074
        CAPTAIN AMERICA: 0.057
        IRON MAN/TONY STARK : 0.037
        WOLVERINE/LOGAN : 0.036
        HAVOK/ALEX SUMMERS : 0.036
        DR. STRANGE/STEPHEN : 0.029
        THING/BENJAMIN J. GR: 0.025
        HAWK: 0.025
        HULK/DR. ROBERT BRUC: 0.024
        MR. FANTASTIC/REED R: 0.024
```

It seems that six heroes from this list (Spider-Man, Captain America, Iron Man, Wolverine, Thing/Benjamin, and Mr. Fantastic) are among those who appeared in the list of the ten heroes with the top degree centralities. However, the top three heroes in the previous list are still occupying the first three positions in the current list.

5.2.4   Eigenvector Centrality

It is proportional to the sum of centrality scores of the neighborhood (e.g., PageRank is a stochastic eigenvector scoring). It is a measure of related influence: who is closest to the most influential people in the graph? A node is important if it is connected to other important nodes. This can mean that a node with a small number of influential contacts may outrank one with a larger number of mediocre contacts (in other words, well-connected people are worth more than ill-connected people).

Example 1
We can use the nx.eigenvector_centrality(g) function from NetworkX library to implement the eigenvector centrality measure against the Krackhardt Kite graph. This measure considers not only the direct neighbors of each node (as done in the degree centrality measure) but also the structure of the network as a whole.

```
In: nx.eigenvector_centrality(g)
Out: {0: 0.3522091841983857,
      1: 0.3522091841983857,
      2: 0.28583482369644964,
      3: 0.4810206692001181,
      4: 0.28583482369644964,
      5: 0.39769090281372055,
      6: 0.39769090281372055,
      7: 0.19586101425312444,
      8: 0.04807425308073237,
      9: 0.011163556091491361}
In:
      print(sorted(nx.eigenvector_centrality(g).items(),key=itemgetter(1)
      , reverse=True))
Out:
      [(3, 0.4810206692001181), (5, 0.39769090281372055), (6,
      0.39769090281372055), (0, 0.3522091841983857), (1,
      0.3522091841983857), (2, 0.28583482369644964), (4,
      0.28583482369644964), (7, 0.19586101425312444), (8,
      0.04807425308073237), (9, 0.011163556091491361)]
```

As you can see, node 3 achieves the highest eigenvector centrality, while node 9 achieves the lowest value. Another observation here is that nodes 5 and 6 that occupy positions two and three, respectively, in this test were also among top three in the preceded centrality tests (degree, closeness, and betweenness). This largely means that they are in a position called boundary spanners. They stand between two graph segments (the core and the periphery) but not being full members of any of them. Both of them connect to node 7, the gate guard of the periphery, and to node 3, the node with the highest degree value.

For an organization, the presence of boundary spanners (also known as bridges)—people having significant ties across organizational and other boundaries—is necessary as they can influence the internal decisions and also represent the organization to the external environment. Boundary spanners have the ability the facilitate information flow and can provide the organization with information from the environment, information that can include critical aspects to the organization's survival and growth. The organization, in turn, can respond to this information and act accordingly. This is why boundary spanners are sometimes called *cosmopolitans*, people with their links with the outside world.

Example 2

Again, we can also check the eigenvector centrality for the hero-to-hero graph and find the ten heroes that have the top eigenvector centralities. For this purpose, we are going to use the nx.eigenvector_centrality method from NetworkX, although there is another implementation from Network which is nx.eigenvector_centrality_numpy. The reason is that the first method is going to solve the eigenvalue faster than the numpy method because of the fixed number of iterations. It is more appropriate for large graphs.

```
In:    eigen_cent = nx.eigenvector_centrality(graph)

In:    all_eigen = sorted(eigen_cent.items(), key=itemgetter(1),
reverse=True)

In:    for node in all_eigen[0:10:]: print "%s: %0.3f" % node
Out:
       CAPTAIN AMERICA: 0.117
       IRON MAN/TONY STARK : 0.103
       SCARLET WITCH/WANDA : 0.101
       THING/BENJAMIN J. GR: 0.101
       SPIDER-MAN/PETER PAR: 0.100
       MR. FANTASTIC/REED R: 0.100
       VISION : 0.099
       HUMAN TORCH/JOHNNY S: 0.099
       WOLVERINE/LOGAN : 0.098
       BEAST/HENRY &HANK& P: 0.095
```

What is interesting in this list is that Captain America and Iron Man are still in the first three positions. However, Spider-Man lost its position and dropped to position five. A new hero, Vision, appears as a new entry at position seven.

5.3 PageRank

PageRank algorithm is the basis of page ranking technique within the Google search engine. It represents the likelihood that a random user following links (e.g., surfing the web) will arrive at a particular page. PageRank scores range between 0 and 1. For example, a PageRank of 0.75 means that there is 75% chance that a person clicking on a random link will be directed to the document with the 0.75 PageRank. Hence, a Web page with higher probability is then considered more important than a Web page with a lower probability. The main difference between PageRank and the three most important centrality metrics (i.e., degree, closeness, and betweenness) is that while these metrics are typically graph-based conceptions such that they are highly dependent on the structural positions of nodes, PageRank represents the flow of influence that propagates through the network. Although PageRank is similar to eigenvector centrality in a way, the algorithm has excellent performance on very large and on dynamic networks.

Example

In this example, we are going to build a fabricated Twitter network with 15 people.
We will then add edges, analyze the network, and, finally, save it.

First, we import the necessary packages:

```
In:  import networkx as nx
     import networkx.algorithms as alg
     import numpy as np
     import matplotlib.pyplot as plt
```

Then, we create the graph object.

```
In: graph = nx.DiGraph()
```

Now, we add 15 nodes representing the 15 people in this network, their ages, and
the number of posts of each individual:

```
In:  graph.add_node('Will', {'age': 22, 'posts': 75})
     graph.add_node('Linda', {'age': 30, 'posts': 12})
     graph.add_node('Smith', {'age': 33, 'posts': 207})
     graph.add_node('Mark', {'age': 29, 'posts': 382})
     graph.add_node('Bill', {'age': 29, 'posts': 107})
     graph.add_node('Jack', {'age': 32, 'posts': 372})
     graph.add_node('Rose', {'age': 19, 'posts': 71})
     graph.add_node('Peter', {'age': 28, 'posts': 111})
     graph.add_node('Hilda', {'age': 27, 'posts': 75})
     graph.add_node('Mary', {'age': 27, 'posts': 56})
     graph.add_node('Glenn', {'age': 34, 'posts': 89})
     graph.add_node('Rick', {'age': 22, 'posts': 121})
     graph.add_node('George', {'age': 31, 'posts': 43})
     graph.add_node('Markus', {'age': 24, 'posts': 113})
     graph.add_node('Alex', {'age': 32, 'posts': 67})
```

Next, we will build the network of followers which consists of who knows who
using the nx.add_edge() method, in addition to the strength of each relationship
which is expressed by the metadata "weight" as follows:

```
In:
graph.add_edge('Will', 'Alex', {'Weight': 3,
'relationship': 'friend'})
graph.add_edge('Will', 'Markus', {'Weight': 2,
'relationship': 'friend'})
graph.add_edge('Will', 'George', {'Weight': 1,
'relationship': 'friend'})
graph.add_edge('Linda', 'Alex', {'Weight': 5,
'relationship': 'friend'})
graph.add_edge('Linda', 'Markus', {'Weight': 4,
'relationship': 'friend'})
graph.add_edge('Linda', 'George', {'Weight': 1,
'relationship': 'friend'})
graph.add_edge('Smith', 'Alex', {'Weight': 3,
'relationship': 'friend'})
graph.add_edge('Smith', 'Markus', {'Weight': 4,
'relationship': 'friend'})
graph.add_edge('Smith', 'George', {'Weight': 4,
'relationship': 'friend'})
graph.add_edge('Mark', 'Alex', {'Weight': 2,
'relationship': 'friend'})
graph.add_edge('Mark', 'Markus', {'Weight': 2,
'relationship': 'friend'})
graph.add_edge('Mark', 'George', {'Weight': 5,
'relationship': 'friend'})
graph.add_edge('Bill', 'Alex', {'Weight': 3,
'relationship': 'friend'})
graph.add_edge('Bill', 'Markus', {'Weight': 2,
'relationship': 'friend'})
graph.add_edge('Bill', 'George', {'Weight': 1,
'relationship': 'friend'})
graph.add_edge('Jack', 'Alex', {'Weight': 1,
'relationship': 'friend'})
graph.add_edge('Jack', 'Markus', {'Weight': 2,
'relationship': 'friend'})
graph.add_edge('Jack', 'George', {'Weight': 1,
'relationship': 'friend'})
graph.add_edge('Rose', 'Alex', {'Weight': 4,
'relationship': 'friend'})
graph.add_edge('Rose', 'Markus', {'Weight': 4,
'relationship': 'friend'})
graph.add_edge('Rose', 'George', {'Weight': 5,
'relationship': 'wife'})
graph.add_edge('Peter', 'Alex', {'Weight': 2,
'relationship': 'friend'})
graph.add_edge('Peter', 'Markus', {'Weight': 2,
'relationship': 'friend'})
graph.add_edge('Peter', 'George', {'Weight': 4,
'relationship': 'friend'})
graph.add_edge('Hilda', 'Alex', {'Weight': 2,
'relationship': 'friend'})
graph.add_edge('Hilda', 'Markus', {'Weight': 2,
'relationship': 'wife'})
graph.add_edge('Hilda', 'George', {'Weight': 1,
'relationship': 'friend'})
graph.add_edge('Mary', 'Alex', {'Weight': 4,
'relationship': 'friend'})
graph.add_edge('Mary', 'Markus', {'Weight': 5,
'relationship': 'friend'})
graph.add_edge('Mary', 'George', {'Weight': 4,
'relationship': 'friend'})
graph.add_edge('Glenn', 'Alex', {'Weight': 3,
'relationship': 'friend'})
graph.add_edge('Glenn', 'Markus', {'Weight': 3,
'relationship': 'friend'})
graph.add_edge('Glenn', 'George', {'Weight': 1,
'relationship': 'friend'})
graph.add_edge('Rick', 'Alex', {'Weight': 5,
'relationship': 'friend'})
graph.add_edge('Rick', 'Markus', {'Weight': 2,
'relationship': 'friend'})
graph.add_edge('Rick', 'George', {'Weight': 1,
'relationship': 'friend'})
```

To retrieve the list of nodes from the graph, simply execute the nx.nodes() method with any parameters:

```
In:  graph.nodes()
Out: ['Rick', 'Alex', 'Glenn', 'Rose', 'Bill', 'Smith',
'Mark', Will', 'Jack', 'George', 'Markus', 'Linda', 'Peter',
'Mary', 'Hilda']
```

While on the other hand, executing nx.nodes(data = True) will return the metadata for each node:

```
In: graph.nodes(data = True)
Out:
[('Rick', {'age': 22, 'posts': 121}),
 ('Alex', {'age': 32, 'posts': 67}),
 ('Glenn', {'age': 34, 'posts': 89}),
 ('Rose', {'age': 19, 'posts': 71}),
 ('Bill', {'age': 29, 'posts': 107}),
 ('Smith', {'age': 33, 'posts': 207}),
 ('Mark', {'age': 29, 'posts': 382}),
 ('Will', {'age': 22, 'posts': 75}),
 ('Jack', {'age': 32, 'posts': 372}),
 ('George', {'age': 31, 'posts': 43}),
 ('Markus', {'age': 24, 'posts': 113}),
 ('Linda', {'age': 30, 'posts': 12}),
 ('Peter', {'age': 28, 'posts': 111}),
 ('Mary', {'age': 27, 'posts': 56}),
 ('Hilda', {'age': 27, 'posts': 75})]

In:    graph.edges()
Out:   [('Rick', 'Markus'), ('Rick', 'Alex'), ('Rick', 'George'), ('Alex',
       Glenn'), ('Alex', 'Rose'), ('Alex', 'Bill'), ('Alex', 'Smith'),
       ('Alex', Mark'), ('Alex', 'Will'), ('Alex', 'Jack'),…]

In:    graph.edges(data=True)
Out:   [('Rick', 'Markus', {'Weight': 2, 'relationship': 'friend'}),
       ('Rick', 'Alex', {'Weight': 5, 'relationship': 'friend'}),
       ('Rick', 'George', {'Weight': 1, 'relationship': 'friend'}),
       ('Alex', 'Glenn', {'Weight': 3, 'relationship': 'friend'}),
       ('Alex', 'Rose', {'Weight': 4, 'relationship': 'friend'}),
       ('Alex', 'Bill', {'Weight': 3, 'relationship': 'friend'}),
       ('Alex', 'Smith', {'Weight': 3, 'relationship': 'friend'}),
       ('Alex', 'Mark', {'Weight': 2, 'relationship': 'friend'}),…]

In:    print"Density of the graph: ", nx.density(graph)
Out:   Density of the graph:  0.171428571429
```

The result shows that our fabricated Twitter network is sparse. This is because the total possible number of edges in our graph, which is defined as n*(n-1)/2, is 105 possible edges. However, we only have 36 edges in the graph, which means only 34.3% of all possible connections.

```
In:     print(nx.info(graph))
Out:    Name:
        Type: DiGraph
        Number of nodes: 15
        Number of edges: 36
        Average in degree:    2.4000
        Average out degree:   2.4000
```

Let's now calculate the degree centrality of nodes in the graph. The degree of a node is the number of connections it has. This includes only the direct connections of that node. NetworkX package provides a function, nx.degree_centrality(), which calculates the ratio of the degree of each node to the maximum possible number of connections in the graph.

```
In:   nx.degree_centrality(graph)
Out:  {'Alex': 0.8571428571428571, 'Bill': 0.21428571428571427, 'George':
      .8571428571428571, 'Glenn': 0.21428571428571427, 'Hilda':
      .21428571428571427, 'Jack': 0.21428571428571427, 'Linda':
      .21428571428571427, 'Mark': 0.21428571428571427, 'Markus':
      .8571428571428571, 'Mary': 0.21428571428571427, 'Peter':
      .21428571428571427,…}
```

If we want to sort the degrees from highest to lowest:

```
In:   centrality = sorted(nx.degree_centrality(graph).items(), key=lambda
      e: e[1], reverse=True)
      print(centrality)

Out:  [('Alex', 0.8571428571428571), ('Markus', 0.8571428571428571),
      ('George', 0.8571428571428571), ('Mary', 0.21428571428571427),
      ('Glenn', 0.21428571428571427), ('Rose', 0.21428571428571427),
      ('Bill', 0.21428571428571427), ('Smith', 0.21428571428571427),
      ('Mark', 0.21428571428571427), ('Will', 0.21428571428571427),
      ('Rick', 0.21428571428571427), ('Linda', 0.21428571428571427),
      ('Hilda', 0.21428571428571427), ('Peter', 0.21428571428571427),
      ('Jack', 0.21428571428571427)]
```

As you can notice, Alex, Markus, and George are the three most connected people in the graph.

Another function from NetworkX, nx. assortativity.average_neighbor_degree(), calculates, for each node, an average of its neighbor's degrees. In the social networking terminology, such a metric would allow to find those who are friends with the most connected people in the network:

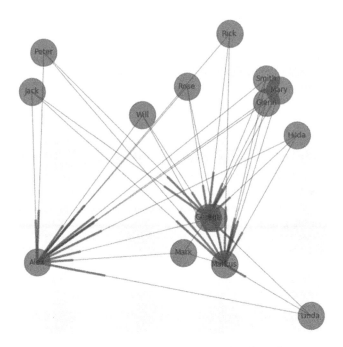

Fig. 5.14 PageRank values of a fabricated Twitter network with 15 people

```
In:   assortativity =
      sorted(nx.assortativity.average_neighbor_degree(graph).items(),key=
      lambda e: e[1], reverse=True)
      print(assortativity)
Out:  [('Peter', 12.0), ('Glenn', 12.0), ('Rose', 12.0), ('Bill', 12.0),
      ('Smith', 12.0), ('Mark', 12.0), ('Will', 12.0), ('Rick', 12.0),
      ('Linda', 12.0), ('Hilda', 12.0), ('Mary', 12.0), ('Jack', 12.0),
      ('Alex', 3.0), ('George', 3.0), ('Markus', 3.0)]
```

It looks that Peter, Glenn, Rose, Bill, Smith, Mark, Will, Rick, Linda, Hilda, Mary, and Jack are all connected to the people with the highest degrees in the network: Alex, Markus, and George.

To draw the graph (Fig. 5.14):

```
In:   plt.figure(figsize=(12,12))
      layout = nx.random_layout(graph)
      nx.draw_networkx(graph, layout, node_color='c', node_size=1000,
       alpha = 0.4)
Out:
```

Running the algorithm for the fabricated Twitter dataset, we get fairly the same result that we got when we applied degree centrality:

```
In:      nx.pagerank(graph)
Out:     {'Alex': 0.17460386794062185,
          'Bill': 0.03968236634817788,
          'George': 0.17460386794062185,
          'Glenn': 0.03968236634817788,
          'Hilda': 0.03968236634817788,
          'Jack': 0.03968236634817788,
          'Linda': 0.03968236634817788,
          'Mark': 0.03968236634817788,
          'Markus': 0.17460386794062185,
          'Mary': 0.03968236634817788,
          'Peter': 0.03968236634817788,
          'Rick': 0.03968236634817788,
          'Rose': 0.03968236634817788,
          'Smith': 0.03968236634817788,
          'Will': 0.03968236634817788}
```

We can further save the graph in the GraphML format that can be read by Gephi visualization package:

```
In:    nx.write_graphml(graph, "…/graph.graphml")
```

Alternatively, in the png file format

```
In:    plt.savefig("…/graph.png")
```

5.4 Neighbors

```
In:  G = nx.Graph()    # or DiGraph, MultiGraph, MultiDiGraph, etc
     G.add_path([0,1,2,3])
     G.neighbors(0)
```

5.5 Bridges

In 1973, Granovetter wrote an article titled "The Strength of the Weak Ties" empha-
sizing the importance that *network bridges* have for the diffusion of information in
social networks. The main argument of Granovetter was that because people's
friends are also likely to be friends, connecting with others who do not know one
another would more likely establish bridges that connect unconnected groups. The
significance of bridges is that they reduce the overall distance between nodes in a
network which in turn speeds up information spread throughout the network.

While most network analysts are concerned with identifying key players and
those located at the center of the network, determining network bridges can be more
at sometimes more important, although often more challenging. Bridges are links
that connect two separate groups, and the anchors for the links are bridge nodes.
People who act as bridges can have particular personality characteristics such as
they are open to hearing new ideas from others. We define individual bridging as
follows:

$$B_i = \frac{\sum_{j=1}^{k} [C - C'_{ij}]}{k} + \frac{\sum_{j=1}^{l} [C - C'_{ji}]}{l}, (i \neq j)$$

where C is cohesion for the observed network, C'_{ij} is cohesion when the links
from i to j is removed, C'_{ji} is cohesion when the links from j to i are removed, and k
and l are the numbers of ties sent and received, respectively.

While betweenness centrality measure has always been used to find central nodes
in bridging positions, bridges are important to find network nodes are not peripheral
or central but have an intermediate position within the network. These nodes may
act as important intermediary relays in the diffusion process and thus should be
strengthened to keep the network cohesive. Nevertheless, there is still some correlation between the two measures such that they may identify the same nodes when the
network structure is uniform. The following figure shows the positions of bridge
and betweenness nodes (Fig. 5.15).

In the above figure, B at the top of the network is a bridge node, whereas D and
E are betweenness nodes. The difference between the two cases is that node B has
two links only and if any of these two links is deleted, the average in distances is
greater than for other nodes. Nodes D and E (among other nodes in the network), on
the other hand, have high and nearly equal betweenness values.

5.6 Which Centrality Algorithm to Use?

So far, we discussed several measures to calculate centrality in networks. While
they represent a valiant approach at understanding the social network forces, there
still exists one question that we want to find an answer: which centrality metric is

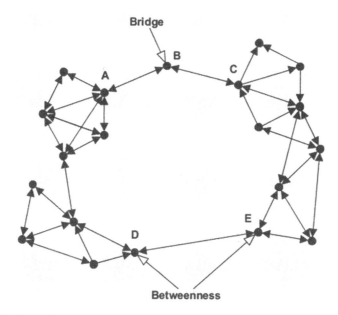

Fig. 5.15 Positions of bridge and betweenness nodes

the best one to use among all? In fact, it all depends on our objectives from conducting the analysis. However, in most cases, all the four measures are applied to have a good understanding of the network structure. Here is a quick summary of the uses of each measure:

1. Degree is a measure of popularity. It determines nodes that can quickly spread information to a localized area.
2. Betweenness is based on the idea that a person is more important if he/she is more intermediary in the network.
3. Closeness is a measure of reach; how fast information will spread to all other nodes from a single node?
4. Eigenvector is a measure of related importance. Who is closest to the most influential people in the graph?

Regarding the three centrality measures (degree, betweenness, and closeness), degree centrality is relatively straightforward and fast and requires only passing over the nodes to compute the number of connected edges. Betweenness and closeness centralities, on the other hand, require the implementation of the minimum spanning tree which, in turn, implements Kruskal's algorithm that has a runtime complexity on the order of $O(E\log E)$, where E is the number of edges. For the eigenvector centrality measure, and because the algorithm must iterate through the neighbors of each node to compute the weighted degree, the algorithm takes on the order of $O(nodes*average\_degree)$ operations. This makes the algorithm very expensive regarding the computational complexity, particularly for very large networks.

Chapter 6
Group-Level Analysis

In this chapter, we are going to present a number of techniques for detecting cohesive groups in networks such as cliques, clustering coefficient, triadic analysis, structural holes, brokerage, transitivity, hierarchical clustering, and blockmodels. All of which are based on how nodes in a network interconnect. However, among all, cohesion and brokerage types of analysis are two major research topics in social network analysis.

6.1 Cohesive Subgroups

Degree centrality, closeness centrality, and betweenness centrality are three main metrics that are used by social network analysis to identify important individuals in a network. Degree centrality looks at the nodes with the highest degrees as the most central nodes in the network. Closeness centrality considers the vertices with the smallest average length of the roads linking one node to other nodes as the main players. Betweenness centrality considers the node with the highest number of shortest paths between pairs of nodes (that run through that node) as the most important individual in a network.

However, they do not tell us what forces make some nodes gather around and build good connections with a central node or what forces tear networks apart and whether a node with a high degree is clustered (i.e., connected strongly to other nodes) or scattered across the network.

Rather than analyzing individual nodes and their connection patterns, we will address entire subgraphs and clusters. Doing so will help us see whether such cohesive groups differ from other network patterns regarding social characteristics, norms, behavior, or density.

Cohesive subgroups are areas with high density of nodes. They are mostly found in undirected networks (compared to directed networks). The importance of

© Springer International Publishing AG 2017
M.Z. Al-Taie, S. Kadry, *Python for Graph and Network Analysis*, Advanced
Information and Knowledge Processing, DOI 10.1007/978-3-319-53004-8_6

identifying cohesive subgroups in networks is that cohesive subgroups are potential social clusters in the network.

Several techniques have been developed to detect cohesive subgroups within a network such as k-core (a subnetwork in which each vertex is connected to at least k vertices in the subnetwork), cliques (maximal connected components, usually have three vertices), and m-slice.

6.2   Cliques

In this section, we are going to analyze the mutual friendships with data from Facebook. Unlike data from Twitter, and some other resources that are more open in nature and we can crawl data over a particular period, Facebook imposes restrictions on personal data access particularly if we are analyzing our social network. This makes Facebook a much more closed community.

NetworkX provides a nice implementation to finding mutual friendships in social networks through the nx.find_cliques() function. We are going to use Facebook data to build a graph of mutual friendship and then use the nx.find_cliques() function to analyze the cliques in the graph.

Finding cliques in a graph, in the computational sense, belongs to a group of problems usually referred to as NP-complete, which means that the combinatorics of the problem grows exponentially as the size of data grows. Finding cliques for very large graphs may take a long time to finish, or the results can be approximated.

The data that we are using for this exercise is compiled by Stanford University (https://snap.stanford.edu/data/egonets-Facebook.html). However, because the dataset is relatively big and finding cliques in a graph has an exponential runtime, we may have memory issues running the entire dataset. Instead, we can extract a small part of the original dataset and use it for our analyses.

Let's check some of the information about this graph:

```
In:     print(nx.info(fb))
Out:
        Name:
        Type: Graph
        Number of nodes: 1820
        Number of edges: 7846
        Average degree:   8.6220
```

Let's see how the graph looks like:

```
In:   fb = nx.read_edgelist("…/facebook_combined_minimized.txt",
      create_using=nx.Graph(), nodetype=int)

In:   cliques = [x for x in nx.find_cliques(fb)]
```

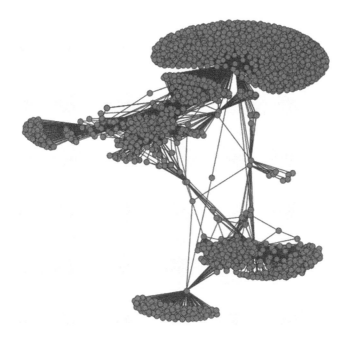

Fig. 6.1 Graphical representation of the Facebook dataset

In edge-list files, the first column is the name of the "from" node, while the second column is the name of the "to" node. There could be some extra information after the second column to signify the strength of tie.

Now, let's draw the network (Fig. 6.1):

```
In:    pos = nx.spring_layout(fb)
       plt.figure(figsize=(12,12))
       plt.axis('off')
       nx.draw_networkx(fb, pos=pos, with_labels=False, node_size=80)

Out:
```

The dataset shows clearly that there are several (around six) large distinct regions. They are not positions on one side of the graph but rather on two sides while at the same time connected by few and long ties.

To take a look at some of the cliques that are present in the graph:

```
In:     cliques
Out:
        [[1, 0, 133, 280, 322, 315, 236],
         [1, 0, 73, 48, 88, 126],
         [1, 0, 73, 48, 299],
         [1, 0, 236, 322, 88],
         [1, 0, 53, 88, 48, 322],
         [1, 0, 53, 315, 322],
         [1, 0, 53, 299, 48],
         [1, 0, 53, 299, 194 346, 92],
         [1, 0, 53, 54, 48],
         [1, 0, 119, 48, 54],
         [1, 0, 119, 280],
         [1, 0, 126, 48, 88, 322],
         [2, 0, 226, 149, 343, 333, 20],
         [2, 0, 226, 149, 343, 326, 312, 115, 20],
         ...]
```

The clique algorithm produces an output that can be quickly interpreted with the naked eye. Let's see how many cliques are there in the graph:

```
In:     n_cliques =len(cliques)
        print(n_cliques)
Out:    10193
```

Let's take a look at the sizes of cliques (with repetition) in the graph:

```
In:     sizes_of_cliques = [len(x) for x in cliques]
        print(sizes_of_cliques)
Out:
        [7, 6, 5, 5, 6, 5, 5, 7, 5, 5, 4, 6, 7, 9, 9, 8, 11, 11, 11, 11, 7,
         8, 7, 4, 4, 5, 10, 4, 4, 4, 5, 5, 5, 5, 3, 4, 6, 6, 5, 5, 7, 7, 5,
         6, 7, 5, 4, 6, 5, 5, 8, 6, 5, 8, 5, 6, 8, 5, 6, 5, 5, 5, 4, 6, 7,
         7, 7, 6, 5, 5, 6, 5, 6, 11, 11, 11, 11, 11, 11, 10, 10, 11, 11, 11,
         11, 11, 11, 4, 6, 6, 6, 7, 5, 5, 8, 10, 10, 8, 10, 10, 10, 10, 9,
         11, 12, 11, 12, 9, 9, 12, 13, 12, 13, 11, 11, 12, 9, 9, 11, 11, 12,
         12, 9, 9, 10, 10, 11,...]

In:     maximum_clique_size = max(sizes_of_cliques)
        print(maximum_clique_size)
Out:    16
```

Let's find the cliques that satisfy the maximum clique size condition which was 16:

```
In:     maximu_cliques = [x for x in cliques if len(c) ==
        maximum_clique_size]
        print(maximu_cliques)
Out:
        [[9, 0, 271, 26, 67, 56, 122, 277, 322, 21, 170, 200, 186, 25, 188,
         323], [9, 0, 271, 26, 67, 56, 122, 277, 322, 21, 170, 200, 186, 25,
         188, 252], [9, 0, 271, 26, 67, 56, 122, 277, 322, 21, 170, 200,
         186, 142, 188, 323], [9, 0, 271, 26, 67, 56, 122, 277, 322, 21,
         170, 200, 186, 142, 188, 252], [9, 0, 271, 26, 67, 56, 122, 277,
         322, 285, 170, 200, 186, 25, 188, 323], [9, 0, 271, 26, 67, 56,
         122, 277, 322, 285, 170, 200, 186, 25, 188, 252],
         ...]
```

And also their number:

```
In:    n_maximum_cluqies = len(maximu_cliques)
       print(n_maximum_cluqies)
Out:   26
```

This means that we have 26 different maximum cliques in the graph, each of which consists of 16 nodes (persons). This means that those 26 variations of 16 people all know one another.

Now, average clique size:

```
In:    average_clique_size = sum(sizes_of_cliques)/n_cliques
       print(average_clique_size)
Out:   8
```

```
In:    maximum_clique_sets = [set(x) for x in maximu_cliques]
In:    print(maximum_clique_sets)
Out:
       [set([0, 322, 67, 200, 9, 170, 271, 323, 277, 186, 56, 25, 26, 188,
       122, 21]), set([0, 322, 67, 200, 9, 170, 271, 252, 277, 186, 56,
       25, 26, 188, 122, 21]), set([0, 322, 67, 200, 9, 170, 142, 271,
       323, 277, 186, 56, 26, 188, 122, 21]),…]
```

Let's use the reduce function to find the nodes (friends) that are common among all the maximum cliques. Remember that we have 26 maximum cliques:

```
In:    friends_in_all_maximum_cliques = list(reduce(lambda x, y:
       x.intersection(y), maximum_clique_sets))
       print(friends_in_all_maximum_cliques)
Out:   [0, 67, 200, 122, 271, 277, 56, 186, 26]
```

Perhaps the most interesting thing is that there are nine people who appeared in all the 26 maximum cliques.

6.3   Clustering Coefficient

Clustering coefficient is the fraction of the node's neighbors that are also neighbors with each other. Neighbors of a node are the set of nodes connected to it by an edge, not including the node itself. This metric can be applied either locally or globally. Locally (for ego networks), it emphasizes the neighborhood of a node, while globally (for entire networks) it is the level of clustering in a graph. However, this measure, if computed at the global level on networks with widely varying densities and multiple cores, would reveal results that are difficult to interpret.

For social networks, this metric is very important as it allows finding the proportion of a person's friends that are also friends with each other. Knowing that would show, for example, the amount of trust people have for each other. In trust networks, messages can easily spread and be sustained.

Example 1

Let's have a look at the following example which is again based on the Krackhardt Kite graph:

```
In:     nx.clustering(g)
Out:
        {0: 0.6666666666666666,
         1: 0.6666666666666666,
         2: 1.0,
         3: 0.5333333333333333,
         4: 1.0,
         5: 0.5,
         6: 0.5,
         7: 0.3333333333333333,
         8: 0.0,
         9: 0.0}
```

The nx.clustering function from NetworkX computed the clustering coefficient for each node in the graph. Higher values of clustering coefficient indicate higher cliquishness which means highly connected segments of the network.

Let's now implement the nx.average_clustering() function which is going to compute the average coefficient for the graph:

```
In:     nx.average_clustering(g)
Out:    0.5199999999999999
```

Example 2

Calculating the clustering coefficient values of each node for the hero network:

```
In:     nx.clustering(graph)
Out:
        {u'QUESADA, JOE': 1.0,
         u'ZEITGEIST II/AXEL CL': 1.0,
         u'LOGA II': 0.7040169133192389,
         u'PIECEMEAL/GILBERT BE': 0.8768873403019745,
         u'BENWAY, DR.': 0.954248366013072,
         u'FRIEDLANDER, SHARON': 0.5136507936507937,
         u'DREAMING CELESTIAL/T': 0.7282282282282282,
         u'MODRED THE MYSTIC': 0.37714776632302405,
         u'THOMAS, DR. STAN': 0.9636363636363636,
         u'FIREWALL/THEARY/MIN ': 0.6688251618871416,
         u'DR. FAUSTUS': 0.6133333333333333,..]
```

Now, we calculate the average network clustering:

```
In:     nx.average_clustering(graph)
Out:    0.7746541217110626
```

Let's see how we can calculate clustering coefficient for a particular node. NetworkX has no direct implementation for this job. We need first to extract the ego network and then apply the average clustering function as follows:

```
In:      ego_net = nx.ego_graph(graph, "QUESADA, JOE")

In:      len(ego_net)
Out:     40

In:      nx.average_clustering(ego_net)
Out:     1.0
```

Joe Quesada has a network of 40 nodes. But why does this hero, Joe Quesada, have a clustering coefficient of 1? Let's check his local network:

```
In:      nx.clustering(ego_net)
Out:
         {'QUESADA, JOE': 1.0, u'ZURI': 1.0, u'GLADIATOR/MELVIN POT': 1.0,
         u'SMITH, KEVIN': 1.0, u'OKOYE': 1.0, u'RALF': 1.0, u'PALMIOTTI,
         JIMMY': 1.0, u'BLAKE, BECKY': 1.0, u'MYSTERIO/QUENTIN BEC': 1.0,
         u'WATSON-PARKER, MARY ': 1.0, u'SPIDER-MAN/PETER PAR': 1.0,
         u'MCKENZIE, LYDIA': 1.0, u'LAMY, KELLY': 1.0, u'URICH, BEN': 1.0,
         u"BLACK PANTHER/T'CHAL": 1.0, u'MR. FANTASTIC/REED R': 1.0,
         u'THING/BENJAMIN J. GR': 1.0, u'QUINN, ASHLEY': 1.0, u'CAPTAIN
         AMERICA': 1.0, u'MALICE V/NAKIA': 1.0, u'NELSON, CANDACE': 1.0,
         u'MARTINEZ, ALITHA': 1.0, u'BUTCH': 1.0, u'EIGHTBALL': 1.0,
         u'DAREDEVIL/MATT MURDO': 1.0, u'ROSS, EVERETT KENNET': 1.0,
         u'POTTER, BETSY BEATTY': 1.0, u'BLACK WIDOW/NATASHA ': 1.0,
         u'EVERETT, BILL': 1.0, u'DAKESIAN, NANCI': 1.0, u'SHARPE,
         ROSALINDE': 1.0, u'NELSON, FRANKLIN FOG': 1.0, u'MILLER, FRANK':
         1.0, u'HUMAN TORCH/JOHNNY S': 1.0, u'OSBORN, LIZ ALLAN': 1.0, u'DR.
         STRANGE/STEPHEN ': 1.0, u'DARLA': 1.0, u'INVISIBLE WOMAN/SUE ':
         1.0, u'PAGE, KAREN': 1.0, u'LEE, STAN': 1.0}
```

This function allows us to find clustering coefficient for each node (hero) in the ego network. Joe Quesada is surrounded by a set of heroes that each has cc = 1 (Fig. 6.2).

```
In:      plt.figure(figsize=(30,30))
         pos = nx.random_layout(ego_net)
         nx.draw_networkx(ego_net, pos, node_size=3000, with_labels=True)
```

6.4 Triadic Analysis

A triad is a subgraph with three nodes: a focal (ego), an altar, and a third node. This structure also includes the ties that are present at the subgraph (if any). It is the smallest graph structure that has more than two nodes (Fig. 6.3).

On the above figure, there are four possible types of undirected triad shapes: closed, open, connected, and unconnected. The graph on the left is a complete triad,

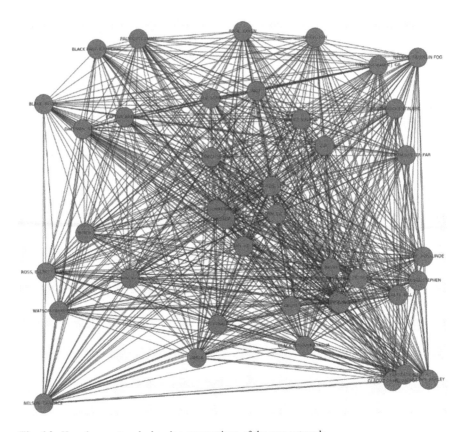

Fig. 6.2 Hero-hero network showing connections of the ego network

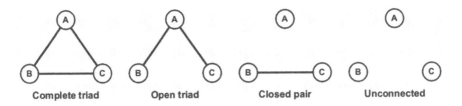

Fig. 6.3 Triad in four cases

a complete subnetwork consisting of three nodes. Nodes A, B, and C are linked to each other via equivalently strong ties. This complete triad is a clique of size three because we cannot add another node from this graph to this subgraph such that it is still complete. However, in the below undirected complete graph, nodes A, B, and C do not establish a clique because we can add node D and the subnetwork is still complete. Nodes A, B, C, and D constitute a clique of size four which is made up of four complete triads (Fig. 6.4).

Fig. 6.4 Complete triad

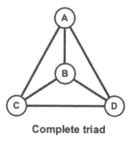

Complete triad

Fig. 6.5 Overlapped triad

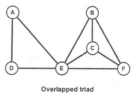

Overlapped triad

The below figure shows a critical characteristic of complete triads, namely, that complete triads can overlap. The complete triad A, B, and C overlaps with another complete triad which is B, C, and E because both of them share node E. In the context of social networks, overlapping cliques are cohesive subgroups that represent overlapping social circles. In fully connected triads, the three people share information and norms, create trust by feedback, and resolve or moderate conflicts by the third person. They behave like a group rather than as a set of individuals. This is different from the dyadic structure in which each two individuals exclusively exchange information and opinions and maintain their relationship while at the same time are not bound by group norms (Fig. 6.5).

For a simple directed graph, there are 16 possible types of triads that may occur. These types are listed in the figure below. Because we consider edges that are both one way and bidirectional, we get 16 variations. Each type is identified by an M-A-N number of three digits and, sometimes, a letter. M, the first digit, indicates the number of mutual positive dyads. A, the second digit, is the number of asymmetric dyads. N, the third digit, is the number of null dyads. A letter that refers to the direction of the asymmetric choices may be added to distinguish between triads with the same M-A-N digits: D → down, U → up, C → cyclic, and T → transitive (in transitive triads, each path of length two is closed by an arc from the starting node to the end node of the path) (Fig. 6.6).

It was found that knowing the types of triads that occur in a directed network can help us infer the overall structure of the network. In other words, by analyzing network triads, we can understand the structure of the overall network.

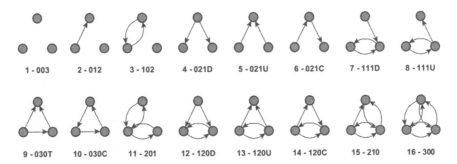

Fig. 6.6 Types of connections in a directed triad

6.5   Structural Holes

A structural hole is a hole (absence of a tie) in the ego network of a node such that two of its neighbors (alter and a third party) cannot connect directly. The person who is connected to people who are themselves not directly connected has the opportunity to mediate between them and profit from this mediation. This person can exploit his or her position to create conflict between the other two to control both of them or settle their disputes. In organizations, a person (expert) who can connect between the jobs of two or more different departments can have more importance and more prestige.

The theory of structural holes was introduced by Ronald Burt in his book "Structural Holes: The Social Structure of Competition" in 1992 as an attempt to study the positional importance of actors in social networks. This idea and several others developed by Ronald Burt opened the way for much thinking on why and how actors get connected to each other and how this can affect their constraints, opportunities, and finally their behavior.

6.6   Brokerage

Certain positions within a network can be heavily involved in the exchange of information, goods, disease, rumor, or services, while others are not. To this end, brokerage focuses on social relations in networks as channels of exchange. It measures ego's potential to induce and exploit competition between actors in a triad. It also measures ego's potential to play subversive roles through creating or exploiting conflicts between other actors to control them.

The brokerage role that an actor can play in a network depends to a great extent on the presence of structural holes: more structural holes mean more brokerage strategies to apply.

Another important concept that is related to brokerage is "aggregate constraint" which is the sum of the dyadic constraint on all the ties of a particular node. The

Fig. 6.7 Ego network
showing possibilities of
brokerage

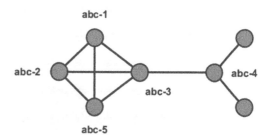

more the aggregate constraint is, the relatively small role a broker can play. The
significance of aggregate constraint is seen in many real-life examples. For instance,
employees with low constraint have more successful jobs than others, while business sectors with low constraint are more profitable.

While structural holes offer great opportunities in incomplete triads, they imply
constraint in complete triads. Because there are no structural holes in complete triads, playing a broker, by the ego, becomes very hard, and any attempt to draw from
any of these ties would create a structural hole around the ego that would disadvantage it while allowing alter to take advantage of. The fewer the structural holes, the
fewer the opportunities to broker. Let's take a look at this figure (Fig. 6.7).

The above figure is an ego network. It consists of the ego "abc-3," the ego's
neighbors, and the ties among them. We can analyze the graph from the perspective
of its triads. For example, the ego (abc-3) has the opportunity to broker between
abc-4 and abc-1 because all the connections between them must go through the ego.
This is also true for all the connections between abc-4 and abc-2 or abc-5. The three
triads, which abc-3 has, give the power to the ego to broker for abc-4. However,
there is also a constraint on the ego in terms of brokering between abc-1, abc-2, and
abc-3. Since these three nodes establish a complete triad, there is no opportunity for
the ego to broker between them.

Comparing the two cases, there is a low constraint projected on the ego to broker
for abc-4 because alter is not connected directly to abc-1, abc-2, or abc-5. However,
there is a high constraint projected on ego to broker between abc-1, abc-2, and abc-5
because these three nodes constitute a complete triad.

Example

In NetworkX, there is a function (triadic_census) that determines the triadic census
of a directed graph. In other words, this function is a count of how many of the 16
possible types of triads are present in the directed graph. It receives one parameter,
a NetworkX directed graph, and returns a dictionary with triad names as keys and
number of occurrences as values. This function has a complexity $O(m)$ where m is
the number of edges in the graph.

In this example, we are going to manipulate the fabricated Twitter (a directed
graph), which we built before, to apply the triadic census function (Fig. 6.8).

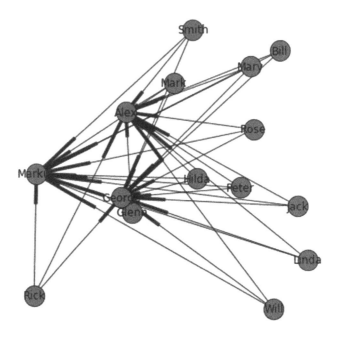

Fig. 6.8 Fabricated Twitter network with 15 nodes

```
In:     print(nx.info(graph))
Out:    Name:
        Type: DiGraph
        Number of nodes: 15
        Number of edges: 36
        Average in degree:   2.4000
        Average out degree:  2.4000

In:     plt.figure(figsize=(8,8))
        layout = nx.random_layout(graph)
        nx.draw_networkx(graph, layout, node_color='r', node_size=500,
        alpha = 0.8)
```

Now, we run the triadic census function:

```
In:     print(nx.triadic_census(graph))

Out:    {'201': 0, '021C': 0, '021D': 36, '210': 0, '120U': 0, '030C': 0,
        '003': 221, '300': 0, '012': 0, '021U': 198, '120D': 0, '102': 0,
        '111U': 0, '030T': 0, '120C': 0, '111D': 0}
```

As we can see, the function has returned a dictionary of triad names and their corresponding number of occurrences. When we match this result with a list of triad types, we find that there are three types of triads that are present in this directed graph: 021D (36 instances), 003 (221 instances), and 021U (198 instances) (Fig. 6.9).

Fig. 6.9 Types of triads
found within the Twitter
network

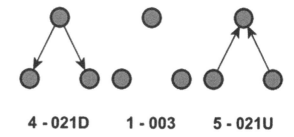

4 - 021D   1 - 003   5 - 021U

Triads 021D and 021U contain pairs of unconnected nodes representing two variants of structural holes. However, ego node cannot benefit from its position as a mediator between the other two nodes because of the asymmetric dyad ties.

The other triad type found in this structure, namely, 003, is found in clusterable networks because it contains nodes which belong to three different clusters.

Having two different types of triads (viz., structural holes and unconnected triads) means that the network is not consistent with one structure. Rather, there are areas with many structural holes (198 + 36 = 234), and there are areas with many unconnected triads (221 instances). Another observation, which can be made here, is that closed triads (code 300), which represent high closure areas, are not present in this network structure.

The ratio between unconnected triads and the structural hole is tiny (0.9) which means that the areas that belong to them are almost equal. These areas can be seen from the sample picture, but for larger networks, it may not be so apparent.

The type of analysis, triad census, in this example, is an instance of a research strategy that is centered on network local structures because it considers only the ties within triads. Triadic analysis, which concentrates on the analysis of triads and their ties in directed graphs, is the basis of statistical models that test hypothesis the motivations that make some nodes, rather than others, establish their ties. It also helps identify the node's role in the network structure.

6.7 Transitivity

Transitivity is a property of edges that allows us to perform triadic closures (closed triples) and make predictions about the node's neighborhood. If node A is connected to node B and node B is connected to node C, then it is likely that node A is also connected to node C. Higher transitivity values indicate higher node's local density.

Completely closed triangles form cliques that can be identified as communities. The nx.transitivity() function, through the nx.triangles() function, computes the number of triangles and divides it by the number of possible triangles in the network.

Example 1

We will use here the hero network.

```
In:     nx.transitivity(graph)
Out:    0.19453974709267596
```

Higher values of clustering coefficients and transitivity may indicate that the graph exhibits the small-world effect, which is one of the properties of social networks. This property predicts that any two individuals are no more than six links away from each other.

Let's also compute the radius (the minimum path length between any two nodes) and the diameter (the maximum path length between any two nodes).

```
In:     nx.radius(graph)
Out:    NetworkXError: Graph not connected: infinite path length

In:     nx.diameter(graph)
Out:    NetworkXError: Graph not connected: infinite path length
```

This is obvious because our graph is disconnected. To work around this issue, let's take a connected component of the graph as follows:

```
In:     sub_graph = nx.connected_component_subgraphs(graph)
```

Let's build a function to find the largest component in that list:

```
In:
    cur_graph = graph

    if not nx.is_connected(cur_graph):
        # get a list of unconnected networks
        sub_graph = nx.connected_component_subgraphs(cur_graph)

        main_graph = sub_graph[0]

        # find the largest network in that list
        for sg in sub_graph:
            if len(sg.nodes()) > len(main_graph.nodes()):
                main_graph = sg

        cur_graph = main_graph
```

The nx.connected_component_subgraphs(graph) function is important for isolating connected components, and it returns an array of graph objects where each object corresponds to one of these connected components:

```
In:      len(graph)
Out:     6426

In:      [len(s) for s in sub_graph]
Out:     [6408, 9, 7, 2]

In:      print(nx.number_connected_components(graph))
Out:     4
```

This shows that our graph consists of 6426 nodes, but the network is split into four disconnected components with the largest of which having 6408 nodes. Each component is, in fact, a subgraph that consists of a set of nodes and the edges that link these nodes. There is no limitation to the number of nodes that a subgraph should contain, as any group of nodes can form a subgraph. Let's now see the distribution of the component sizes (Fig. 6.10).

Of the four components, three are of size <10. There are no isolated components (isolates are node components with degree zero) in this graph, although we have three components with a low degree (9, 7, and 2). In this graph, we have one giant subgraph—a significant component that fills most of the network and occupies about 99.7% of it.

In real network applications, such as the Internet, it is important to have a component that fills most of the network. This component would provide a path throughout the Internet network and can provide computer-to-computer communications to consumers. Such a network structure, in which the network is divided into one large component and several other small components, is found typically in undirected networks.

Let's see how we can extract the subgraphs that satisfy a particular condition corresponding to a minimum number of node degree:

```
In:      [len(s) for s in nx.connected_component_subgraphs(graph) if len(s)
         > 5]
Out:     [6408, 9, 7]
```

Fig. 6.10 Distribution of the component sizes of the hero network

This means that there are four components of size >5. In this particular case, we can treat the giant component as the whole network.

Let us now calculate the diameter and radius of the largest of this component:

```
In:     sub_graph = sub_graph[0]

In:     nx.diameter(sub_graph)
Out:

In:     nx.radius(sub_graph)
Out:
```

Implementing nx.connected_components(graph), on the other hand, will produce a list of nodes for each component of the graph.

It has become possible now to calculate eccentricity: the max shortest path length from each node in the network at a time it was not possible to make this calculation when the graph consists of more than one component.

```
In:     ecc = nx.eccentricity(sub_graph)
Out:
```

Example 2

In this example, we will consider the Facebook network.

```
In:     fb = nx.read_edgelist("…/facebook_combined_minimized.txt",
        create_using=nx.Graph(), nodetype=int)

In:     nx.radius(fb)
Out:    3

In:     nx.diameter(fb)
Out:    5

In:     print(nx.info(fb))
Out:    Name:
        Type: Graph
        Number of nodes: 1820
        Number of edges: 7846
        Average degree:    8.6220

In:     nx.number_connected_components(fb)
Out:    1

In:     len(fb)
Out:    1820

In:     sub_graph = nx.connected_component_subgraphs(fb)

In:     [len(s) for s in sub_graph]
Ou:     [1820]
```

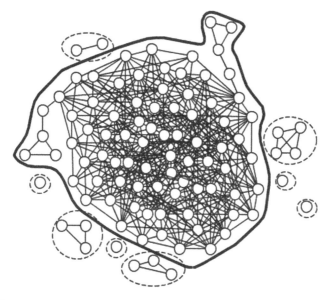

Fig. 6.11 Coreness

6.8 Coreness

A node's coreness (core number) is c if it belongs to a c-core but not $(c + 1)$-core. It helps to determine how strongly the node is connected to the network. Calculating coreness leads to the classification of nodes into several layers, which is helpful for visualization (Fig. 6.11).

6.9 Overlapping Communities

Do disjoint non-overlapping communities make sense in empirical social networks? Overlapping communities may exist at different levels of granularity (Fig. 6.12).

Distinct "non-overlapping" communities rarely exist at large scales in many empirical networks. Communities overlap pervasively, making it impossible to partition the networks without splitting communities (Fig. 6.13).

There is no built-in support for overlapping algorithms, but we can use the MOSES tool to analyze graphs represented as edge lists. MOSES is the scalable approach for identifying highly overlapping communities. (1) Randomly select an edge, and greedily expand a community around the edge to optimize an objective function. (2) Delete "poor quality" communities. (3) Fine-tune communities by re-assigning individual nodes.

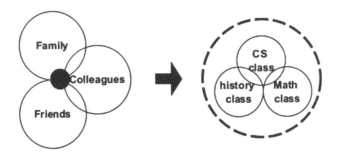

Fig. 6.12 Overlapping communities

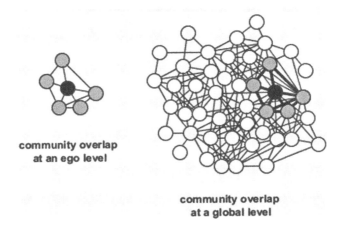

Fig. 6.13 Community overlapping at both ego and global levels

6.10   Dynamic Community Finding

In many SNA tasks, we will want to analyze how communities in the network form
and evolve over time. Often, perform this analysis in an "offline" manner by examining successive snapshots of the network (Fig. 6.14).

We can characterize dynamic communities regarding key life cycle events: (1)
birth and death of communities, (2) expansion and contraction of communities, and
(3) merging and splitting of communities. The mechanism is as follows: apply community finding algorithm to each snapshot of the graph, then match newly generated
"step communities" with those that have been identified in the past.

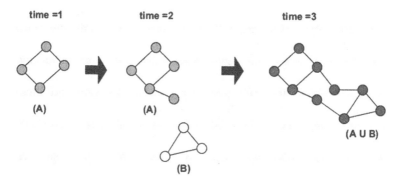

Fig. 6.14 Small community evolving in three steps

6.11   M-Slice

M-slice is a maximal sub-network that has lines with a multiplicity equal to (or greater than) m, as well as the vertices incident with these lines. The goal is to identify cohesive subgroups, which depends on line multiplicity. This measure was first introduced by John Scott, who first called it "m-core." Based on this measure, isolated nodes are defined as 0-slice, since they share nothing. However, m-slice does not guarantee that all vertices within the m-slice component are connected at a minimum level of line multiplicity. Instead, the elements of the m-slice are considered cohesive rather than the m-slice itself.

6.12   K-Cores

K-cores is a connected component of a network which is obtained by repeatedly deleting all the nodes whose degree is less than k until no more such nodes exist. This process results in all k-core nodes to have at least a degree of k. The k-cores measure helps to identify where core clusters are. The largest value of k, for which a k-core exists, is called "degeneracy" of the network.

6.13   Community Detection

The community is a subgraph of a network in which nodes are connected to each other more densely than to the outside.

Finding communities in networks, where vertices are organized into clusters in a way that many edges join vertices of the same cluster and few edges join vertices of different clusters, has become an active research area for scientists and researchers.

Many algorithms have been proposed for community detection including the spectral bisection algorithm (which is based on the properties of the spectrum of the Laplacian matrix) and the Kernighan-Lin Algorithm (which is one of the earliest approaches proposed and is still frequently used but mostly in combination with other methods. It is based on the idea of partitioning electronic circuits onto boards.). Other popular methods for graph partitioning include the geometric algorithm, level-structure partitioning, and multilevel algorithms.

Community detection involves the identification of groups of nodes which share common properties and/or play a similar role within the graph (Fortunato 2010). Such groups have a dense node-node connection while low dense node-node connections with other groups (Fig. 6.15).

6.13.1   Graph Partitioning

Graph partitioning aims at dividing graph nodes into some pre-specified groups of nodes to optimize a criterion related to the number of edges cut. Min-cut is a traditional approach of graph partitioning that involves minimizing number (or weight) of edges cut by the partition. More advanced approaches use normalized cuts and apply multilevel strategies to scale to large graphs (Fig. 6.16).

6.13.2   Hierarchical Clustering

Social sciences have adopted a different approach to finding communities which is based on developing a measure of similarity between pairs of vertices with the help of some similarity measure.

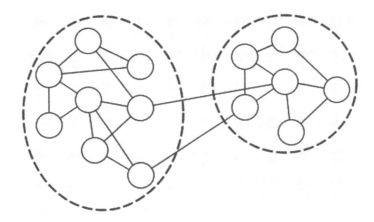

Fig. 6.15 Identification of communities in networks

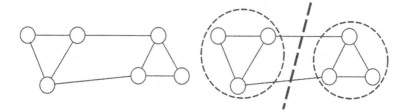

Fig. 6.16 Graph partitioning

Fig. 6.17 Hierarchical
clustering

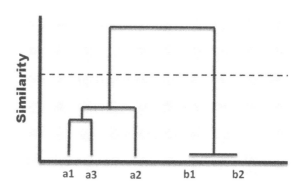

Hierarchical clustering is a statistical data clustering technique that can be used to cluster pairs of nodes which are nearly structural equivalent into positions. It allows for checking the structural features of social networks. First, the algorithm groups nodes that are most similar. Then, it groups the next pair of nodes or clusters that are most similar. This is repeated until all nodes have been joined. The algorithm approaches the problem of clustering by developing a binary tree-based data structure called the dendrogram (Fig. 6.17).

In the above illustration (dendrogram) which visualizes the results of hierarchical clustering, nodes b1 and b2 are first joined because they are completely similar (dissimilarity = zero). Next, nodes a1 and a3 are clustered because their dissimilarity is tiny. Then, node a2 is added to the cluster of a1 and a2. In the fourth and final step of the clustering process, this cluster is merged with the cluster of nodes (b1 and b2). In the dendrogram, the higher a branch is, the more dissimilar two nodes or clusters are at the moment when they are joined.

If we want to split the same dendrogram into its primary nodes, we reverse the order on which we built the dendrogram. First, we divide the cluster that joins the two clusters (a1, a3, and a2) and (b1 and b2). Next, we split the cluster that contains nodes a1, a3, and a2. Finally, we split the cluster that contains nodes a1 and a2. A general rule for splitting dendrograms is that clusters are split at the place or places where the branches make significant jumps. This means that we should first detect clusters of nodes that are structural equivalent or near equivalent.

Example 1

The following simple recursive program shows how we can build a hierarchy of graphs (a dendrogram-like structure) using NetworkX. The code is provided by Joel [https://stackoverflow.com/users/2966723/joel] with some modifications.

```
In:
    import networkx as nx
    def hierarchy_pos(G, root, width=1., vert_gap = 0.2, vert_loc = 0,
    xcenter = 0.5 ):
        def h_recur(G, root, width=1., vert_gap = 0.2, vert_loc = 0,
    xcenter = 0.5,
                       pos = None, parent = None, parsed = [] ):
            if(root not in parsed):
                parsed.append(root)
                if pos == None:
                    pos = {root:(xcenter,vert_loc)}
                else:
                    pos[root] = (xcenter, vert_loc)
                neighbors = G.neighbors(root)
                if parent != None:
                    neighbors.remove(parent)
                if len(neighbors)!=0:
                    dx = width/len(neighbors)
                    nextx = xcenter - width/2 - dx/2
                    for neighbor in neighbors:
                        nextx += dx
                        pos = h_recur(G,neighbor, width = dx, vert_gap =
    vert_gap, vert_loc = vert_loc-vert_gap, xcenter=nextx, pos=pos,
    parent = root, parsed = parsed)
            return pos

        return h_recur(G, root, width=1., vert_gap = 0.2, vert_loc = 0,
    xcenter = 0.5)
```

Some notes about the definition of the above function:

1. If there is a cycle that is reachable from the root, then the result will not be a hierarchy.
2. G: the graph.
3. Root: the root node of the current branch.
4. Width: horizontal space allocated for this branch—avoids overlap with other branches.
5. vert_gap: gap between levels of hierarchy.
6. vert_loc: vertical location of root.
7. Xcenter: horizontal location of the root.

This is an example on how to use the above code (Fig. 6.18):

```
In:
    G=nx.Graph()
    G.add_edges_from([(1,2), (1,3), (1,4), (2,5), (2,6), (2,7), (3,8),
    (3,9), (4,10), (5,11), (5,12), (6,13), (6, 14), (7, 15), (7, 16), (8,
    17), (8, 18), (9, 19), (9, 20), (10, 21), (10,22)])
    pos = hierarchy_pos(G,1)
    nx.draw(G, pos=pos, with_labels=True, node_size= 500,
    node_color='orange')
```

```
Out:
```

Fig. 6.18 Hierarchy of
graphs

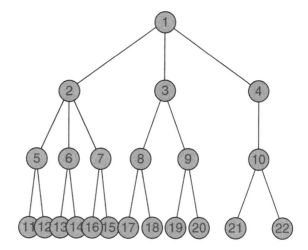

However, how can we compute the distance between two clusters? In fact, there
are several methods to solve these issues. Let's define three of them:

- *Single linkage*. This method merges two clusters having the smallest minimum
  pairwise distance.
- *Average linkage*. This method merges two clusters having the smallest average
  pairwise distance.
- *Complete linkage*. This method merges two clusters having the smallest maximum pairwise distance.

Hierarchical clustering can be achieved in two different ways, namely, bottom-
up (agglomerative) and top-down (divisive) clustering. Even though both of these
two approaches utilize the concept of dendrogram to perform clustering, they might
result in entirely different results depending on the criterion used during the clustering process:

1. *Agglomerative*. A bottom-up approach is used to build the tree, starting from the
   individual data points and moving on toward merging clusters until ending up
   with one final cluster. Merging clusters incorporates the use of one of the merging techniques in a way that is supposed to achieve a trade-off between efficiency
   and quality. Such techniques include single linkage, sampled linkage, all-pairs
   linkage, and centroid linkage. Starting with each node as assigned to one separate
   cluster, a bottom-up approach is applied where the most similar pairs of clusters
   are merged at each stage.
2. *Divisive*. A top-down approach is used to partition the data into smaller components forming a tree-like structure eventually. Starting with a single cluster that
   contains all nodes in the network, a top-down approach is applied where a chosen cluster is split into two sub-clusters at each stage.

Example 2

Let's see how hierarchical clustering works by taking this example using simple data. Because so far NetworkX has no direct implementation for hierarchical clustering, we will use a hierarchical clustering in SciPy package. The code is originally written by Taro Sato [http://okomestudio.net/] (Fig. 6.19).

In:
```
import matplotlib.pyplot as plt
from scipy.cluster.hierarchy import dendrogram, linkage
from numpy import array
import numpy as np


mat = array([[184, 222, 177, 216,31,
              45, 123, 128, 200,
              129, 121, 203,
              46, 83,
              83])

dist_mat = mat

linkage_matrix = linkage(dist_mat, 'single')
print linkage_matrix

plt.figure(101)
plt.subplot(1, 2, 1)
plt.title("ascending")
dendrogram(linkage_matrix,
           color_threshold=1,
           truncate_mode='lastp',
           labels=array(['a', 'b', 'c', 'd', 'e', 'f']),
           distance_sort='ascending')

plt.subplot(1, 2, 2)
plt.title("descending")
dendrogram(linkage_matrix,
           color_threshold=1,
           truncate_mode='lastp',
           labels=array(['a', 'b', 'c', 'd', 'e', 'f']),
           distance_sort='descending')

def make_fake_data():
    amp = 1000.
    x = []
    y = []
    for i in range(0, 10):
        s = 20
        x.append(np.random.normal(30, s))
        y.append(np.random.normal(30, s))
    for i in range(0, 20):
        s = 2
        x.append(np.random.normal(150, s))
        y.append(np.random.normal(150, s))
    for i in range(0, 10):
        s = 5
        x.append(np.random.normal(-20, s))
        y.append(np.random.normal(50, s))
```

```
            plt.figure(1)
            plt.title('fake data')
            plt.scatter(x, y)

            d = []
            for i in range(len(x)- 1):
                for j in range(i+1, len(x)-1):
                    d.append(np.sqrt(((x[i]- x[j])**2 + (y[i]-y[j])**2)))
            return d

    mat = make_fake_data()


    plt.figure(102)
    plt.title("Three Clusters")

    linkage_matrix = linkage(mat, 'single')
    print "three clusters"
    print linkage_matrix

    dendrogram(linkage_matrix,
               truncate_mode='lastp',
               color_threshold=1,
               show_leaf_counts=True)

    plt.show()
```

Out:
```
    [[  1.    2.    45.    2.]
     [  3.    4.    46.    2.]
     [  5.    7.    83.    3.]
     [  6.    8.   121.    5.]
     [  0.    9.   177.    6.]]
    three clusters
    [[  15.         22.          0.33632604    2.          ]
     [  20.         26.          0.39356172    2.          ]
     [  10.         18.          0.62552494    2.          ]
     [  17.         29.          0.80644649    2.          ]
     [  25.         42.          0.85853812    3.          ]
     [  16.         40.          0.8586993     3.          ]
     [  11.         12.          0.91381892    2.          ]
     [  39.         44.          1.06065447    5.          ]
     [  21.         27.          1.08475839    2.          ]
     [  28.         43.          1.12965956    4.          ]
     [  19.         46.          1.26167457    6.          ]
      ...
```

Fig. 6.19 Hierarchical
clustering using Scipy

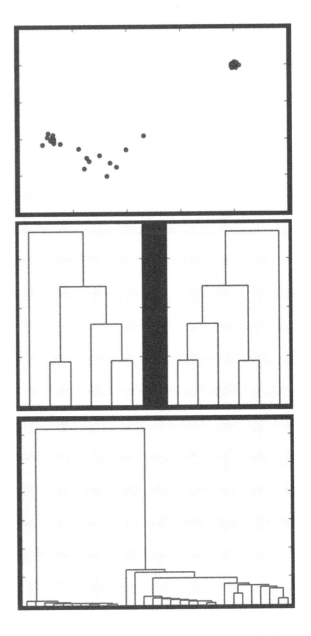

The example uses matplotlib.pyplot to plot the results, dendrogram and linkage
from scipy.cluster.hierarchy to build the dendrograms and define the linkage method,
array from numpy to define the distance matrix, and numpy package to generate
random numbers. The example uses the "single-" linkage method to define the distance between clusters using two implementations: ascending and descending. We
can try other options such as average, complete, or weighted. They will provide

completely different results (although the number of clusters which is three will remain the same).

make_fake_data() is a function that generates random data for the sake of this example. Let's look at a sample data that is generated from executing this function:

```
In:    mat
Out:   [45.245034231790527,
        52.318030166215507,
        62.669312651126731,
        61.023428681366973,
        44.312064158396517,
        58.228649487002663,
        74.700976436821762,
        35.956497691214871,
        33.423710737357311,
        206.50594326367511,
        206.46813737653895,
        207.32596327946229,
        210.9789592576071,
        206.63628599779912,
        ...]

In:    len(mat)
Out:   741
```

6.14 Blockmodels

A blockmodel is a reduced version of a larger network in which nodes are collapsed based on a given partition of the node set. Each partition of nodes (block), in this new network, is represented as a single node. Similarly, the relationships between nodes in the original network are aggregated to connect between blocks in the new network. The importance of a blockmodel is that it is an effective device to describe the overall structure of a network and the position of each node in this structure. The process of deriving a smaller network from a larger network is called blockmodeling.

So, blockmodeling is a technique that is very similar to hierarchical clustering. It is designed to detect some structural features of social networks such as cohesions, core/periphery, and ranking. While grouping nodes into clusters and determining the relations between these clusters, blockmodeling uses matrices (e.g., adjacency matrices) to perform computations and data visualization. It is a flexible and efficient method to analyze small dense social networks.

While techniques such as centrality measures are based on the structural positions of nodes, blockmodeling provides a different perspective on other concepts. Built on different structural concepts, equivalence and positions, which are related to theoretical concepts of social role and role sets, blockmodeling describes the social roles and associated patterns of ties in the network at large. However, other techniques are still valid to work on large or sparse networks.

The implementation of blockmodeling requires that we either already know the blockmodel of a network (the assignment of nodes to classes and the image matrix that specify the permitted types of the block) or that there is a network that we want to find the blockmodel that captures the structure of the network. In the following examples, we will assume that we know the blockmodel of these networks.

Example 1
There is a nice implementation for blockmodels in networkx. nx.blockmodel(G, partition). The function returns a reduced graph constructed using the generalized blockmodeling technique. It accepts, as parameters, G, a NetworkX graph or DiGraph; partition, a non-overlapping partition of nodes; and multigraph (optional), Boolean value. On the other hand, the function returns a blockmodel, a NetworkX graph object (Figs. 6.20 and 6.21).

```
In:     G=nx.path_graph(10)
        nx.draw_networkx(G)

Out:
```

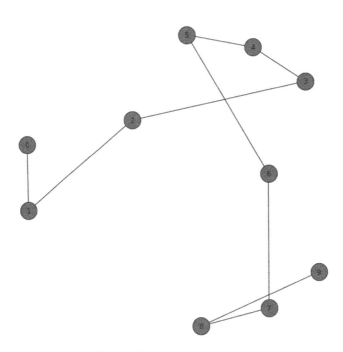

Fig. 6.20 Simple path graph with ten nodes

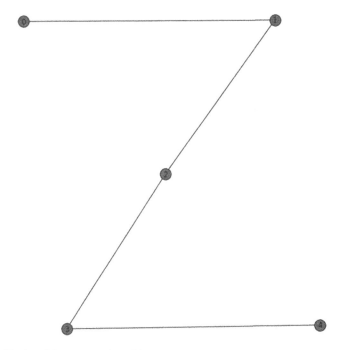

Fig. 6.21 Blockmodel representation of the path graph

```
In:      partition = [[0,1],[2,3],[4,5], [6, 7], [8, 9]]
         M = nx.blockmodel(G,partition)

In:      nx.draw_networkx(M)
Out:
```

We can, alternatively, change the blockmodeling process such that it generates two blocks rather than five (Fig. 6.22):

```
In:      partition = [[0,1,2,3],[4,5, 6, 7, 8, 9]]
         M = nx.blockmodel(G,partition)

In:      nx.draw_networkx(M, node_size=800)
Out:
```

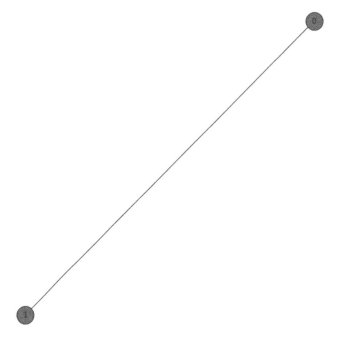

Fig. 6.22 Blockmodel representation of the path graph (with two-block)

Example 2

The following code (which is borrowed from https://networkx.github.io) uses the "Hartford, CT drug users network" dataset. Let's first import the dataset and then plot it (Figs. 6.23 and 6.24):

```
In:    print(nx.info(G))
Out:   Name:
       Type: Graph
       Number of nodes: 212
       Number of edges: 284
       Average degree:   2.6792

In:    nx.draw_networkx(G)
Out:
```

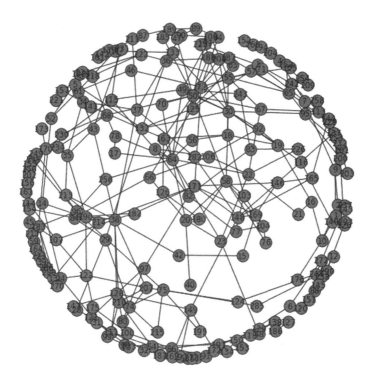

Fig. 6.23 Hartford, CT drug users network

Fig. 6.24 Blockmodel
representation of the
Hartford, CT drug users
network

In:

```python
#!/usr/bin/env python
# encoding: utf-8
"""
Example of creating a block model using the blockmodel function in
NX.  Data used is the Hartford, CT drug users network:
@article{,
  title = {Social Networks of Drug Users in {High-Risk} Sites:
Finding the Connections},
  volume = {6},
  shorttitle = {Social Networks of Drug Users in {High-Risk} Sites},
  url = {http://dx.doi.org/10.1023/A:1015457400897},
  doi = {10.1023/A:1015457400897},
  number = {2},
  journal = {{AIDS} and Behavior},
  author = {Margaret R. Weeks and Scott Clair and Stephen P. Borgatti
and Kim Radda and Jean J. Schensul},
  month = jun,
  year = {2002},
  pages = {193--206}
}
"""
# Authors:  Drew Conway <drew.conway@nyu.edu>, Aric Hagberg
<hagberg@lanl.gov>

from collections import defaultdict
import networkx as nx
import numpy
from scipy.cluster import hierarchy
from scipy.spatial import distance
import matplotlib.pyplot as plt
def create_hc(G):
    """Creates hierarchical cluster of graph G from distance
matrix"""
        path_length=nx.all_pairs_shortest_path_length(G)
        distances=numpy.zeros((len(G),len(G)))
        for u,p in path_length.items():
            for v,d in p.items():
                distances[u      ][v]=d
        # Create hierarchical cluster
        Y=distance.squareform(distances)
        Z=hierarchy.complete(Y)  # Creates HC using farthest point
linkage
        # This partition selection is arbitrary, for illustrive purposes
        membership=list(hierarchy.fcluster(Z,t=1.15))
        # Create collection of lists for blockmodel
        partition=defaultdict(list)
        for n,p in zip(list(range(len(G))),membership):
            partition[p].append(n)
        return list(partition.values())
```

```
if __n   ame__ == '__main__':

G=nx.read_edgelist("C:/Users/Zuhair/Desktop/hartford_drug.edgelist")

    # Extract largest connected component into graph H
    H = next(nx.connected_component_subgraphs(G))
    # Makes life easier to have consecutively labeled integer nodes
    H=nx.convert_node_labels_to_integers(H)
    # Create paritions with hierarchical clustering
    partitions=create_hc(H)
    # Build blockmodel graph
    BM=nx.blockmodel(H,partitions)

    # Draw original graph
    pos=nx.spring_layout(H,iterations=100)
    fig=plt.figure(1,figsize=(6,10))
    ax=fig.add_subplot(222)
    nx.draw(H,pos,with_labels=False,node_size=10)
    plt.xlim(0,1)
    plt.ylim(0,1)

    # Draw block model with weighted edges and nodes sized by number
of internal nodes
    node_size=[BM.node[x]['nnodes']*10 for x in BM.nodes()]
    edge_width=[(2*d['weight']) for (u,v,d) in BM.edges(data=True)]
    # Set positions to mean of positions of internal nodes from
original graph
    posBM={}
    for n in BM:
        xy=numpy.array([pos[u] for u in BM.node[n]['graph']])
        posBM[n]=xy.mean(axis=0)
    ax=fig.add_subplot(666)

nx.draw(BM,posBM,node_size=node_size,width=edge_width,with_labels=Fal
se)
    plt.xlim(0,1)
    plt.ylim(0,1)
    plt.axis('off')
Out:
```

6.14.1 Modularity Optimization

Modularity is a measure of the structure of the graph (it is not node oriented) and quantity that characterizes how good a given community structure is in dividing the network. It is provided as follows:

$$Q = \frac{|E_{in}| - |E_{in-R}|}{|E|}$$

where $|E_{in}|$ is the number of links connecting nodes that belong to the same community and $|E_{in-R}|$ is estimated $|E_{in}|$ if links were random.

Modularity, which was first introduced by Newman and Girvan in 2003, is the most used technique. It attempted to achieve a first understanding of how clustering is done. This technique consists of two steps. The first one, *divisive,* includes iteratively removing edges from the network to finally breaking it out into communities. In the second step, *recalculation,* the betweenness scores are re-calculated when any edge is removed. These two processes are repeated until the maximum global modularity score is reached. The result is a set of subnetworks of nodes that are densely intra-connected while sparsely interconnected.

Modularity scores range between -0.5 and $+1.0$ where high values indicate good division.

6.15   The Louvain Method

The Louvain method is an algorithm for community detection in large networks, developed by Vincent Blondel, Jean-Loup Guillaume, Renaud Lambiotte, and Etienne Lefebvre. It shows how a network can divide naturally into groups of nodes in which dense connections are formed within groups and sparser connections are formed between groups. Based on the concept of modularity maximization, the Louvain method is an efficient greedy approach that scales to large graphs with up to 10^9 edges (or one million nodes). The running time of this algorithm is $O(n \log n)$.

The algorithm works as follows: (1) By optimizing modularity locally on all the nodes, small communities of nodes are found. (2) Small communities are then grouped into one node, and the first step is repeated. For weighted graphs, modularity is defined as

$$Q = \frac{1}{2m} \cdot \sum_{i,j} \left[a_{ij} - \frac{k_i k_j}{2m} \right] \cdot \delta(c_i c_j)$$

where a_{ij} is the edge weight between nodes i and j; k_i and k_j are the sum of the weights of the ties connected to nodes i and j, respectively; m is the sum of all tie weights in the graph; c_i and c_j are the communities of the nodes; and δ is the Kronecker delta that is used to check whether a pair of samples belong to the same community or not. The value of Q is between -1 and $+1$ where optimizing this value can theoretically produce better grouping of nodes. But because going through all possible iterations of the nodes into groups is not practical, heuristic algorithms are used.

Reference

Fortunato S (2010) Community detection in graphs. Phys Rep 486(3):75–174

Chapter 7
Network-Level Analysis

In this chapter, we are going to study graphs and networks as a whole, which is different from what we had done in the previous chapters when we analyzed graphs at the node level and the group level. Hence, this chapter addresses concepts such as components and isolates, cores and periphery, network density, shortest paths, reciprocity, affiliation networks and two-mode networks, and homophily.

7.1 Components/Isolates

A component is a set of actors that are internally connected but are disconnected from the rest of vertices in the network. When a vertex is isolated from other vertices, it simply becomes isolate.

7.2 Core/Periphery

In network cores, members are densely tied to each other. However, in a periphery nodes are more linked to the core members than to each other.

Some researchers studied the world economic system in 1974 and stopped at concepts related to network structure such as core and periphery. They showed that the countries in the middle of the model (core countries) such as the USA, Japan, and the Western countries were the wealthy countries. On the other hand, the countries in the periphery of the model such as Bolivia, Panama, and Nicaragua are the underdeveloped countries. Another sphere, called semi-periphery, intermediates the communication between the core and the periphery.

Researchers have found that actors with many ties (actors at the network core) and actors with only a few ties (actors at the network periphery) have constrained

© Springer International Publishing AG 2017   147
M.Z. Al-Taie, S. Kadry, *Python for Graph and Network Analysis*, Advanced
Information and Knowledge Processing, DOI 10.1007/978-3-319-53004-8_7

and predictable behavioral patterns. However, actors with only some ties do not have predictable behaviors, which depend mainly on whom they are connected to.

7.3 Density

Density is defined as the number of network edges divided by the maximum possible number of edges between nodes in that network. All values of density are between 0 and 1. This measure is useful in exploring some network dynamics such as the speed at which information diffuses between nodes and the levels of social capital and social constraints that network nodes have.

Example

```
In:      import networkx as nx
         %matplotlib inline
         import matplotlib.pyplot as plt
```

Let us first build our network from NetworkX Karate Club graph and then calculate the density:

```
In:      g = nx.karate_club_graph()
         nx.density(g)
Out:     0.13903743315508021
```

Let us build our ego network and again calculate the density:

```
In:      ego = nx.ego_graph(g, 8)
         nx.density(ego)
Out:     0.6666666666666666
```

As you can imagine, our Karate Club network is not very dense as a whole compared to node eight network which is very dense and cliquish.

Now, let us calculate the density of the hero network:

```
In:      nx.density(graph)
Out:     0.00810031232553549
```

7.4   Shortest Path

$L(i,j)$ is the length shortest path(s) between i and j. Usually, the computation of shortest paths is done with Dijkstra's algorithm. The longest distance in a graph is called the diameter, and it represents the longest shortest path over all pairs of nodes in the network (or Max eccentricity in the network). The goal of network diameter measure is to index the extensiveness of the network, which means how far apart the two furthest nodes in the network are from each other. Radius is the min eccentricity in the network. In social networks, less dense networks will have a larger diameter compared to more dense networks. Additionally, the average shortest path over all pairs of nodes is an interesting measure as it can characterize how large the world represented by the network is, where a small length implies that the network is well connected globally.

Example
Let us do some calculations over the Karate Club graph:

```
In:    nx.shortest_path(g, 0, 8)
Out:   [0, 8]
In:    nx.shortest_path_length(g, 0, 8)
Out:   1
In:    nx.average_shortest_path_length(g)
Out:   2.408199643493761
```

The nx.all_pairs_shortest_path() function will allow us to see a list of the shortest paths for every node in the graph:

```
In:    print(nx.all_pairs_shortest_path(g))
Out:   {0: {0: [0], 1: [0, 1], 2: [0, 2], 3: [0, 3], 4: [0, 4], 5: [0, 5],
       6: [0, 6], 7: [0, 7], 8: [0, 8], 9: [0, 2, 9], 10: [0, 10], 11: [0,
       11], 12: [0, 12], 13: [0, 13], 14: [0, 2, 32, 14], 15: [0, 2, 32,
       15], 16: [0, 5, 16], 17: [0, 17], 18: [0, 2, 32, 18], 19: [0, 19],
       20: [0, 2, 32, 20], 21: [0, 21], 22: [0, 2, 32, 22], 23: [0, 2, 32,
       23], 24: [0, 31, 24], 25: [0, 31, 25], 26: [0, 8, 33, 26], 27: [0,
       2, 27], 28: [0, 2, 28], 29: [0, 2, 32, 29],…}
```

We can also find the shortest paths between all the nodes and a particular node in the graph:

```
In:    print(nx.all_pairs_shortest_path(g)[1])
Out:   {0: [1, 0], 1: [1], 2: [1, 2], 3: [1, 3], 4: [1, 0, 4], 5: [1, 0,
       5], 6: [1, 0, 6], 7: [1, 7], 8: [1, 0, 8], 9: [1, 2, 9], 10: [1, 0,
       10], 11: [1, 0, 11], 12: [1, 0, 12], 13: [1, 13], 14: [1, 2, 32,
       14], 15: [1, 2, 32, 15], 16: [1, 0, 5, 16], 17: [1, 17], 18: [1, 2,
       32, 18], 19: [1, 19], 20: [1, 2, 32, 20], 21: [1, 21], 22: [1, 2,
       32, 22], 23: [1, 2, 32, 23], 24: [1, 2, 27, 24], 25: [1, 0, 31,
       25], 26: [1, 13, 33, 26], 27: [1, 2, 27], 28: [1, 2, 28], 29: [1,
       2, 32, 29], 30: [1, 30], 31: [1, 0, 31], 32: [1, 2, 32], 33: [1,
       13, 33]}
```

Calculating graph diameter is critical for social networks because nodes send and receive communication messages, and hence calculating diameters helps to provide an understanding of how information flows or propagates. In normalized graphs, all edges have the same opportunity receiving information, provided that they are located at the same distance from the information source. On the other hand, in weighted graphs where edges can represent the frequency of individual communications (in addition to other things), edge weights can tell us how quickly information would flow from one node to another.

Let us first calculate graph diameter, which can be defined as the maximum eccentricity (the eccentricity of a node v is the maximum distance from v to all other nodes in g):

```
In:     nx.diameter(g)
Out:    5

In:     print(nx.eccentricity(g))
Out:    {0: 3, 1: 3, 2: 3, 3: 3, 4: 4, 5: 4, 6: 4, 7: 4, 8: 3, 9: 4, 10: 4,
        11: 4, 12: 4, 13: 3, 14: 5, 15: 5, 16: 5, 17: 4, 18: 5, 19: 3, 20:
        5, 21: 4, 22: 5, 23: 5, 24: 4, 25: 4, 26: 5, 27: 4, 28: 4, 29: 5,
        30: 4, 31: 3, 32: 4, 33: 4}
```

The nx.eccentricity() method from NetworkX package returns a dictionary of eccentricity values keyed by the node.

Another way to calculate graph diameter:

```
In:     eccentricity = nx.eccentricity(g)
        print(max(eccentricity.values()))
Out:    5

In:     radius = nx.radius(g)
        print(radius)
Out:    3

In:     print(min(eccentricity.values()))
Out:    3
```

7.5 Reciprocity

Reciprocity of a directed graph is the ratio of the number of edges (relationships) pointing in both directions to the total number of relationships in the graph (or social network).

$$R = | (u,v) \in G | (v,u) \in G | / | (u,v) \in G |.$$

The reciprocity of a single node u is defined similarly. It is the ratio of the number of edges in both directions to the total number of edges attached to node u. This means that reciprocity is not defined for isolated nodes. In such cases, this function will return none.

This measure can only be calculated for directed graphs (such as Twitter) where you can follow others although others may not necessarily follow you. On the other hand, Facebook friendship network is always undirected.

To calculate the reciprocity of the hero graph:

```
In:    und_graph = graph.to_undirected()
       reciprocity =
       float(nx.number_of_edges(und_graph)/nx.number_of_edges(graph))
       print(reciprocity)
Out:   1.0
```

Because the hero network in undirected, it gives a reciprocity result of 1.0.

7.6 Affiliation Networks

Affiliation networks are networks that consist of at least two different sets of nodes (called actors and events) in a way that ties (also called affiliations) connect nodes from different sets only. They are called affiliation networks to express node multi-membership or multi-participation (Fig. 7.1).

People can be members of more than one group, usually known as co-membership. Co-membership in a group or an event can be an indicator of some social tie since co-participation networks allow social ties to develop which, in turn, helps innovation, information, news, and others to flow in the network.

Co-membership in a group or an event produces affiliation data that are used to represent the connectivity between two entities from two different sets. A binary

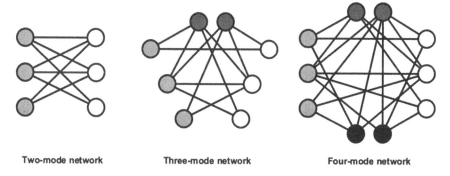

Two-mode network   Three-mode network   Four-mode network

Fig. 7.1 Different types of affiliation networks

Table 7.1 Actor-event relationship

	Event 1	Event 2	Event 3
Actor 1	1	0	0
Actor 2	1	0	1

Fig. 7.2 Simplified people-to-club network

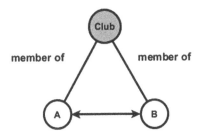

value (0 or 1) means a binary relationship. For example, the ego can be a member of some social community, a participant in some event, or none of them. The following matrix shows an example of affiliation data that represent the relationships between some actors who attended some events. If the actor attended the event, we insert one; otherwise, we insert 0. The larger the number of times some people attend the same event (also called rate of participation), the more likely these people would interact with each other and develop later some relationship (Table 7.1).

In the above table, Actor 1 and Actor 2 are both a participant in Event 1. This makes them more likely to develop relationships over time. This likelihood can become higher if the number of events they attend together (rate of participation) increases (Fig. 7.2).

In the above simplified people-to-club network, persons A and B are members of the same club. Essentially, this graph is an open triad with a structural hole. Since A and B are members of the same club, we can slightly infer that they know each other and that the triad is closed. This inference can be consolidated if we were able to know that A and B were members of the same club at the same time, used to attend it during the same working hours, or practiced the same kind of activity.

7.7   Two-Mode Networks

Affiliation graphs are sometimes called two-mode, bipartite, or bimodal network. They are represented by bipartite graphs $B = (V1, V2, E)$, where $V1$ and $V2$ are the two different sets of nodes, while E is a set of edges that only connect nodes from opposite sets. For example, a dataset can contain data about employees connected to managers or managers connected to the board of directors. Besides organizations, this also applies to gangs, political parties, social clubs, and many others.

We can say that two-mode networks are the networks that consist of only two sets of nodes. Structurally, these networks are different from one-mode networks in which all nodes belong to one set, and hence each node can be related to each other node (Fig. 7.3).

In the above graph, we have two sets of nodes *V1* (has four nodes) and *V2* (has three nodes). They are connected through a set of edges *E* (has six edges) that connect only nodes from different sets.

Some network measures (such as completeness and density) should be computed for two-mode networks in a way that is distinct from the way that is applied for one-mode networks. Completeness, for example, which is defined as the maximum number of lines in a network, is much higher in one-mode networks as for two-mode networks. This is because any node on one-mode networks can connect to some or all other nodes in the same network. In contrast, nodes from one set in two-mode networks can only connect to form the other set. Moreover, because of this observation, density, which is computed as the number of edges in a network divided by the maximum possible number of edges in the same network, is higher for one-mode networks compared to two-mode networks. Hence, the techniques used for analyzing one-mode networks cannot be applied to two-mode networks. So what can we do? A good solution should involve a technique that does not modify or change the meaning of two-mode networks.

It is possible to change the two-mode network into a one-mode network. This is done by dividing the nodes into two disjoint sets such that edges are no more connecting nodes from different sets. This results in two networks of one mode. Standard analysis techniques can be applied next to analyze the new network (Fig. 7.4).

In the above graph, the two sets of nodes, *V1* and *V2*, were connected through a set of edges, *E*. Converting the graph into two separate graphs would create a pair of one-mode networks. Edges now are connecting between nodes of the same set rather than nodes from different sets. The establishment of the new edges is done based on node co-membership or co-participation in the original network. The

Fig. 7.3 Two-mode network

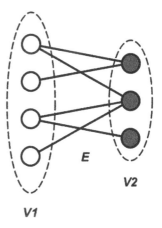

Fig. 7.4 Two-mode
network to two one-mode
networks

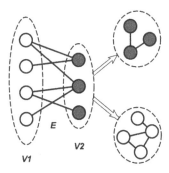

resulting one-mode network is usually dense and contains many cliques. Techniques for analyzing cliques or complete subnetworks (such as blockmodeling, hierarchical clustering, islands, k-cores, and m-slice) can be applied here to detect cohesive groups. This is in fact because the induced networks are networks of similarities or correlations.

In many cases, the derived network is not simple. This means that it may contain loops. Multiple lines (more than one edge or arc connecting between a pair of nodes) can be replaced by a single line to obtain a valued network (a network in which lines have values) with a line value that indicates the strength of the relationship (number of lines) between this pair of nodes. Such a line value is referred to as line multiplicity. The larger the value of line multiplicity (interlocks between two nodes), the stronger or more cohesive their tie is.

Deriving a one-mode network from the two-mode network would help discover social relationships, never were able to be discovered before, between actors of the same set.

7.8 Homophily

Joint membership of a social community often means that there is a similarity in some interests. For example, people who are members of a chess club are very likely to have similar professions, interests, or even social status. It is a matter of the number of shared intensity that induces the degree of similarity between people.

One of the benefits obtained when deriving one-mode networks from a two-mode network is the identification of interaction patterns, at least more often than with dissimilar people, between similar people. This phenomenon is known as homophily (a Greek word means love of the similar).

Coined by Lazarsfeld and Merton in 1954, this phenomenon goes beyond network patterns such as degree, distance, density, and other metrics that only concern network structure. In precise, in social networks, nodes (people) tend to be more often linked to other nodes that are similar to themselves than to nodes that are less similar in characteristics. This mixing pattern (assortativity) is based on personal characteristics such as age, profession, gender, hobby, political view, and many others.

Homophily can impact behavior and welfare in a variety of ways. Ideas, attitudes, and social connections of people can be influenced by being a member of some social, cultural, recreational, or scientific community. For instance, workers' decisions of whether to drop out of the labor force are impacted by homophily in the way that such decisions depend on to a great extent on a worker's friends and colleagues.

Back to the preceding people-to-club example, an extended version is a two-mode (affiliation) network connecting people to the clubs they joined. Deriving a one-mode network from the original network would create a person-to-person network and a club-to-club network. The first network is more interesting to us as it shows who are likely to be connected to who. A list of suggested friends can be created and introduced to each person based on interconnections in the person-to-person network. Not only that but a list of suggested preferences can also be created to tell people what their counterparts like or prefer.

Example 1

In this example, we are going to build a very simple bipartite graph. We need to import NetworkX and bipartite from networkx.algorithms. Bipartite requires that NetworkX version 1.5 or newer be installed.

We will start with an empty undirected graph (directed graphs can also be considered). When adding edges to nodes, we need to keep track of which set each node belongs to and make sure we do not add edges between nodes of the same set. It is conventional to use a node attribute named "bipartite" with values 0 or 1 to identify each set of nodes (Fig. 7.5).

```
In:    import networkx as nx
       from networkx.algorithms import bipartite

In:    B = nx.Graph()
       B.add_nodes_from[1,2,3,4,5,6,7,8], bipartite=0)
       B.add_nodes_from(['a','b','c','d','e'], bipartite=1)

In:    nx.draw_networkx(B, node_color='y', node_size=800)
Out:
```

Let us add some edges between nodes from the two different sets:

```
In:    B.add_edges_from([(1,'a'), (1,'b'), (2,'b'), (2,'c'), (3,'c'),
       (3,'d'), (4, 'd'), (4, 'e'),(5, 'd'), (5, 'e'), (6, 'd'), (7,
       'd'),(8, 'e'), (8, 'a')])
```

Let us draw the graph (Fig. 7.6):

```
In:    nx.draw_networkx(B, node_colcr='y', node_size=800)
Out:
```

Let us check if the graph is bipartite (a two-mode network):

```
In:     bipartite.is_bipartite(B)
Out:    True
```

Let us check if the graph is connected:

```
In:     nx.is_connected(B)
Out:    True
```

Let us check the node sets of the bipartite graph:

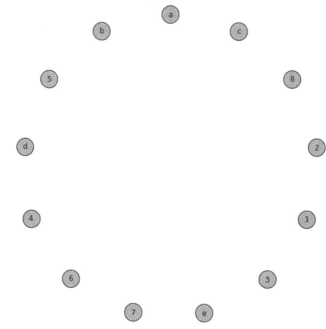

Fig. 7.5 Bipartite graph with no edges between nodes

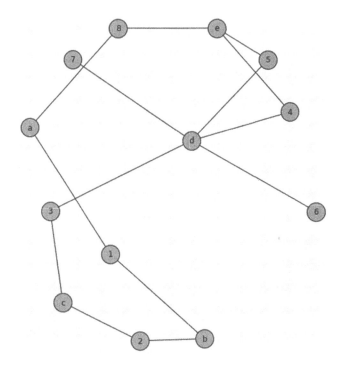

Fig. 7.6 Bipartite graph with edges between nodes

```
In:       bipartite.sets(B)
Out:      ({'a', 'b', 'c', 'd', 'e'}, {1, 2, 3, 4, 5, 6, 7, 8})


In:       bottom_nodes, top_nodes = bipartite.sets(B)
          list(bottom_nodes)
Out:      ['a', 'c', 'b', 'e', 'd']

In:       list(top_nodes)
Out:      [1, 2, 3, 4, 5, 6, 7, 8]
```

There is another method to get the two node sets, which is based on the "bipartite" node attribute.

```
In:       top_nodes = set(n for n,d in B.nodes(data=True) if
          d['bipartite']==0)
          bottom_nodes = set(B) - top_nodes

In:       list(top_nodes)
Out:      [1, 2, 3, 4, 5, 6, 7, 8]

In:       list(bottom_nodes)
Out:      ['a', 'c', 'b', 'e', 'd']
```

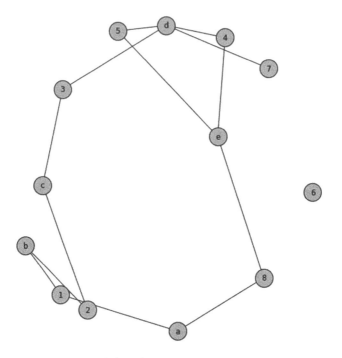

Fig. 7.7 Bipartite graph with a missing edge

Let us check the graph density:

```
In:     bipartite.density(B, nodes)
Out:    0.3333333333333333
```

Let us calculate the rounded density (two positions after the dot) of the graph:

```
In:     round(bipartite.density(B, bottom_nodes),2)
Out:    0.35
```

Let us see what happens if we remove one of the edges (Fig. 7.7):

```
In:     B.remove_edge(6,'d')
        nx.is_connected(B)
Out:    False

In:     nx.draw_networkx(B, node_color='y', node_size=800)
Out:
```

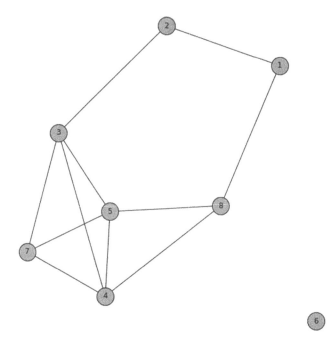

Fig. 7.8 One-mode network from the first set of nodes

Example 2

In this example, we will continue our work from the previous example by converting the current bipartite graph into two one-mode networks. The bipartite.projected_graph() function returns the projection of B on one of its node sets:

```
In:   G = bipartite.projected_graph(B, top_nodes)
```

The new one-mode network is called G. It consists of the first set of nodes, namely, top nodes. Let us check some details of this graph (Fig. 7.8):

```
In:   G.edges()
Out:  [(1, 8), (1, 2), (2, 3), (3, 4), (3, 5), (3, 7), (4, 8), (4, 5),
      (4, 7), (5, 8), (5, 7)]

In:   G.nodes()
Out:  [1, 2, 3, 4, 5, 6, 7, 8]

In:   nx.draw_networkx(G, node_color='y', node_size=800)
Out:
```

The second one-mode network consists of nodes from the other set (bottom nodes) (Fig. 7.9).

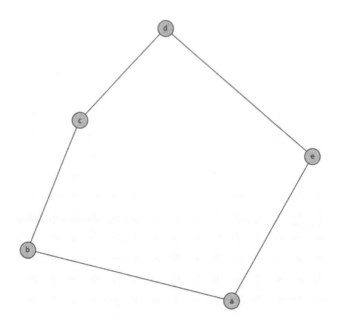

Fig. 7.9 One-mode network from the second set of nodes

```
In:    G = bipartite.projected_graph(B, bottom_nodes)
       G.nodes()
Out:   ['a', 'c', 'b', 'e', 'd']

In:    print(G.edges())
Out:   [('a', 'b'), ('a', 'e'), ('c', 'b'), ('c', 'd'), ('e', 'd')]


In:    nx.draw_networkx(G, node_color='y', node_ize=800)
Out:
```

After deriving one-mode networks from the two-mode network, we can go further from this point and apply standard network analysis techniques. We can use hierarchical clustering, clique identification, or blockmodeling to detect cohesive subgroups. We can also use betweenness centrality or triad census to find boundary spanners (or bridges). Centrality measures can also be applied to find central nodes.

Example 3
There is another method that creates complete bipartite graphs straight from NetworkX library (Fig. 7.10):

```
In:    B = nx.complete_bipartite_graph(3, 2)
In:    nx.draw_networkx(B, nx.random_layout(B), node_size = 800)
Out:
```

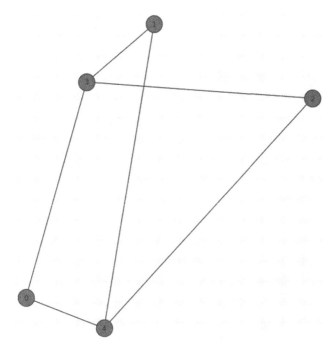

Fig. 7.10 Complete bipartite graph with two sets of nodes (3, 2)

```
In:     X=set([0,1,2])
        bipartite.density(B,X)
Out:    1.0

In:     Y=set([3,4])
        bipartite.density(B,Y)
Out:    1.0
```

Example 4
In this example, we will build a bipartite random graph (Fig. 7.11):

```
In:   randB = bipartite.random_graph(15, 10, 0.5)
      nx.draw_networkx(randB, nx.random_layout(randB), node_size=800,
      node_color='magenta', edge_color='orange')
Out:
```

Probably, the above figure does not really look like a bipartite graph. Let us do
something about it (Fig. 7.12):

Fig. 7.11 Bipartite random graph with two sets of nodes (15, 10)

```
In:     X, Y = bipartite.sets(randB)
        position = dict()
        position.update( (n, (1, i)) for i, n in enumerate(X) ) # put nodes
        from X at x=1
        position.update( (n, (2, i)) for i, n in enumerate(Y) ) # put nodes
        from Y at x=2
        nx.draw(randB, pos=pos, with_labels=True, node_size=800,
        node_color='magenta')
        plt.show()
```

Let us see some information about this graph:

```
In:     print(nx.info(randB))
Out:    Name: fast_gnp_random_graph(30,50,0.5)
        Type: Graph
        Number of nodes: 80
        Number of edges: 726
        Average degree:  18.1500
```

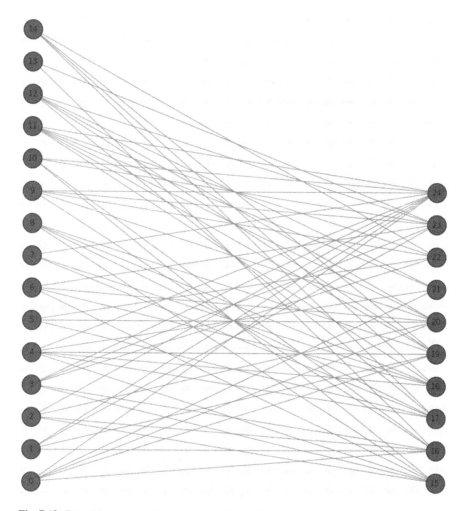

Fig. 7.12 Repositioning of nodes of the bipartite graph

Let us check if the graph is really bipartite:

```
In:    nx.is_bipartite(randB)
Out:   True
```

Let us check the nodes of both sets:

```
In:    randB_top = set(n for n,d in randB.nodes(data=True) if
       d['bipartite']==0)
       randB_bottom = set(randB) - randB_top

In:    print(list(randB_top))
Out:   [0, 1, 2, 3, 4, 5, 6, 7, 8, 9, 10, 11, 12, 13, 14, 15, 16, 17, 18,
       19, 20, 21, 22, 23, 24, 25, 26, 27, 28, 29]


In:    print(list(randB_bottom))
Out:   [30, 31, 32, 33, 34, 35, 36, 37, 38, 39, 40, 41, 42, 43, 44, 45,
       46, 47, 48, 49, 50, 51, 52, 53, 54, 55, 56, 57, 58, 59, 60, 61, 62,
       63, 64, 65, 66, 67, 68, 69, 70, 71, 72, 73, 74, 75, 76, 77, 78, 79]
```

In this graph, we have two sets of nodes 1 and 0. Let us see how we can predict the group of any node. For this purpose, we are going to use another function, color(), which returns a dictionary keyed by node with a 1 or 0 as data for each node color:

```
In:    c = bipartite.color(randB)
       print(c)
Out:   {0: 1, 1: 1, 2: 1, 3: 1, 4: 1, 5: 1, 6: 1, 7: 1, 8: 1, 9: 1, 10: 1,
       11: 1, 12: 1, 13: 1, 14: 1, 15: 1, 16: 1, 17: 1, 18: 1, 19: 1, 20:
       1, 21: 1, 22: 1, 23: 1, 24: 1, 25: 1, 26: 1, 27: 1, 28: 1, 29: 1,
       30: 0, 31: 0, 32: 0, 33: 0, 34: 0, 35: 0, 36: 0, 37: 0, 38: 0, 39:
       0, 40: 0, 41: 0, 42: 0, 43: 0, 44: 0, 45: 0, 46: 0, 47: 0, 48: 0,
       49: 0, 50: 0, 51: 0, 52: 0, 53: 0, 54: 0, 55: 0, 56: 0, 57: 0, 58:
       0, 59: 0, 60: 0, 61: 0, 62: 0, 63: 0, 64: 0, 65: 0, 66: 0, 67: 0,
       68: 0, 69: 0, 70: 0, 71: 0, 72: 0, 73: 0, 74: 0, 75: 0, 76: 0, 77:
       0, 78: 0, 79: 0}
```

Let us check the group for one of the nodes:

```
In:    nx.set_node_attributes(randB, 'bipartite', c)
In:    print(randB.node[30]['bipartite'])
Out:   0
```

Chapter 8
Information Diffusion in Social Networks

In this chapter, we will discuss concepts of information diffusion in social networks. We are interested in knowing how a piece of information (knowledge) is spread through a network. These may be computer viruses spreading on the Internet or a network of computers, diseases through a social network, or rumors and ideas through a social network. Information diffusion methods are commonly used in viral marketing, in collaborative filtering systems, in emergency management, in community detection, and in the study of citation networks.

We will present, in detail, two general types of information diffusion in social networks: diffusion of innovation and epidemics. Diffusion of innovation is studied in many fields, but in this chapter, we are considering it only from a social network perspective. Other kinds of information diffusion that are not included in this chapter include herd behavior and information cascades.

8.1 Diffusion

Diffusion is the process by which information is spread from one place to another through interactions. It is a field that encompasses techniques from a plethora of sciences and techniques from different fields such as sociology, epidemiology, and ethnography. Of course, everyone is interested in not getting infected by a contagious disease. The diffusion process involves three main elements as follows:

1. *Sender.* A sender (or a group of senders) is responsible for initiating the diffusion process.
2. *Receiver.* A receiver (or a group of receivers) receives the diffusion information from the sender. Commonly, the number of receivers is higher than the number of senders.

M.Z. Al-Taie, S. Kadry, *Python for Graph and Network Analysis*, Advanced Information and Knowledge Processing, DOI 10.1007/978-3-319-53004-8_8

3. *Medium*. This is the channel through which the diffusion information is sent from the sender to the receiver. This can be TV, newspaper, social media (e.g., a tweet on Twitter), social ties, air (in the case of a disease spreading process), etc.

From a network point of view: how is the diffusion process handed over? In fact, social relations play a significant role. They are the channels by which social contagion and persuasion are done. Particularly, the structural positions of persons and their personal characteristics make some people more ready to adopt the innovation than others. Networks with different patterns of connection have different properties regarding how things are propagated, which have significant implications for interventions into, for example, rumor propagation.

A diffusion starts with an adopter (or a few number of adopters) who spreads the innovation to others. Innovation typically represents newness, it is not the same thing as invention, it is both a process and an outcome, and it involves discontinuous change.

Those who adopt early are often too innovative to be influential in a local network. They contaminate their contacts who in turn contaminate their contacts and so on. The more people a person is linked to, the greater the chances that that person will adopt the innovation. At a larger scale, and since communities are interlinked, it is very likely that an innovation jumps from one community to another via boundary spanners (or bridges) and starts over diffusing again. It is a characteristic of social networks.

However, any diffusion process can be expedited, delayed, or even stopped if it is discovered that the product (e.g., a video, an audio, a book, etc.) is faulty, and it should be fixed and then released again. This process is called an *intervention*. Intervention can be achieved via several methods such as stopping the production of the product, limiting the distribution of the product, restricting the exposure to the product, reducing the interest in the product, or reducing interactions within the population. In any way, intervention processes can cause damage to the work of small companies as many customers will no longer trust the products that are produced by these companies.

8.2   Contagion

Another important concept that is sometimes used alongside diffusion is *contagion*. It describes how a disease can spread rapidly in a network. In its biological form, contagion requires close physical contact to propagate. However, at times, merely being in the same place where infections/germs are present is enough to spread the disease. Even in these cases, there are limiting factors that influence whether an exposed person will catch a disease or not such as age, gender, immunity, length, weight, overall health, the strength of the virus, and timing of contact with the infected nodes.

Contagion models are similar to diffusion (or social contagion) models but with some distinctions between the two as follows:

- Contagion is often viewed through the lens of infectious diseases (although sometimes it used to describe different phenomena in the marketing and social spaces). Diffusion, on the other hand, is the process or state of something (an idea, innovation, rumor, digital property, and so on) spreading more widely.
- Contagion is commonly initiated by an infection, while diffusion is initiated by traditional media, word of mouth, advertising, or industry events, just to name a few.
- While contagion does not condition a direct contact between the victim and an infected body, diffusion, on the other hand, is concerned with the spread of ideas, innovations, and other concepts that require some direct contact (not necessarily a physical contact).
- Contagion is dependent on physical proximity, regardless whether others are part of a person's social or professional network. The case is different for diffusion which requires some social contact or influence to take root.
- Contagion models do not involve processes such as decision making, in which an individual makes a decision whether to become infected or not because contagion is considered a random natural process. In diffusion models, diffusion making is typically involved. For example, when a rumor is spreading, the set of individuals who receive this rumor would decide whether they are interested in spreading it to their neighbors or not.

In the following section, we will discuss diffusion on innovations, which explains how new ideas and practices spread within and between communities.

8.3 Diffusion of Innovation

Diffusion of innovation, which is an important social process, describes how an innovation (e.g., product, music, video, fad, opinion, or attitude) is handed over from one node (person) to another in a social network over time. It is the theory that has used network principles and perspectives most extensively and has provided the theoretical underpinnings to research how networks influence behavior and behavior change.

New ideas or practices enter communities from external sources such as mass media, labor exchanges, technological innovations, cosmopolitan contact, and many others. However, they can also be originated in the same community where they diffuse. In all these cases, diffusions are done through interpersonal contact networks.

Having roots in anthropology, economics, geography, sociology, marketing, epidemiology, and others, diffusion of innovation is critical for many groups. For example, organizations are interested in the diffusion of information, and opinion makers are interested in the adoption of new products.

Hundreds of studies were conducted in the 1950s and the early 1960s to find answers to why and how innovations spread, the reasons for the diffusion process, why some people adopt a new idea, why some people adopt earlier than others who wait for a substantial amount of time before adopting, and the rate at which an innovation spreads. The research in the field refreshed in recent years with the advent of more sophisticated network models and technology.

It should be noted that diffusion of innovation typically takes a long time. For example, the telephone took decades before it became popular in the USA, and the videocassette recorder (or VCR) took a long time to populate. The reason for the diffusion is that it is often the result of a network structure, which for one reason or another inhibits diffusions. In contrast, the advent of computer technologies and mobile communications has accelerated that rate at which information and other products are adopted. For example, Facebook took only a few years to reach millions of users.

8.4 Adoption of Innovations

An adoption is a decision taken by a person (or persons) that includes a full use of innovation as the best course of action available. An important observation is that adoption does not happen right after a person first someone learns about a new product. Rather, five stage processes of adoption are included in the theory of diffusion of innovations. These stages can be adopted for use in market segmentation and for use in measuring the progress toward behavior change.

1. Becoming aware of the product (but with a limited size of information)
2. Starting to find more information about the product
3. Making a decision to adopt it
4. Trying the product
5. Fully adopting the product

8.5 Diffusion of Innovation Models

Social networks allow many new ideas and practices to spread through interpersonal contacts that largely consist of interpersonal communication. Many of the things that spread can be modeled in similar ways. Hence, knowing how diseases, for example, propagate through networks will also let us know how the rest of things propagate. For example, in retail marketing, information such as reviews and feedback are spread at no cost to the seller via what is called viral marketing. Such a mechanism of information spread is important because it provides a way to know how people are looking at the particular product.

The social media, in most communities, are central to the spreading of information. Hence, several models have been proposed to represent the process in which the social media is responsible for the spread of information (or mass communication). In this section, we will consider one of these models, which is the two-step flow model (or the multistep flow model) which was proposed by Elihu Katz, a professor of communication at the University of Pennsylvania. In cooperation with Paul Lazarsfeld and Robert Merton, Professor Katz pioneered many innovations particularly on how radio and television influenced mass audiences.

8.6   Two-Step Flow Model

The *two-step flow* model is one of the simplest models to model the diffusion of the innovation process. The model considered the effects of mass media on many behaviors including customer behavior and voting patterns. The model proposed the idea that media effects were mediated by interpersonal influence, as opposed a previous view that the mass media had impacted people directly.

In this model, which is consistent with a network approach, mass communication processes are divided into two stages.

1. In the first stage, mass media influence opinion leaders. Opinion leaders are individuals who commonly have a high influence on the behavior of the rest in his or her network by virtue of age, experience, charisma, embeddedness, and perceived homophily. They use both types of ties (silent social relations and advice and friendship relations) to tell their contacts about how important the innovation is and why they should adopt it.
2. In the second stage, opinion leaders influence potential adopters. People who were exposed to messages from mass media did not automatically believe them. Because opinion leaders were more exposed to media and more aware of the current trends, they were able to persuade others to follow their views with the help of media communications to support their arguments. This model, and because media influence opinion leaders who in turn influence others that in turn influence others, can also be called a *multistep flow model* (Fig. 8.1).

Here is a simple example of how the two-step flow model works. Suppose that a company is trying to market a new software program in a network of users. The company did not allocate enough budget for the campaign. So, what it did is that it selected a small number of users (shop owners) to promote its software, shop owners who are central in their local networks with the highest in-degree scores. They can talk to their friends, customers, and social connections about the software and why it is a new trend in the market. Their immediate neighbors, in turn, will talk about the product to their neighbors and so on until finally the news about the product is spread to a large population of users in the network. In this simple example, the company is the mass media, shop owners are the opinion leaders, and neighbors are the potential adopters.

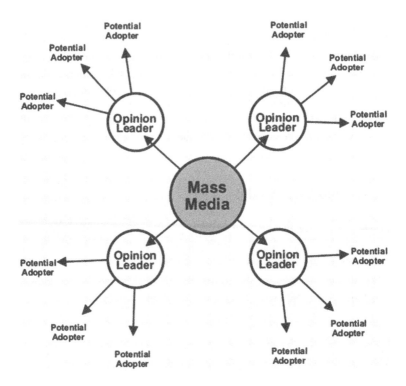

Fig. 8.1 Two-step flow model

8.7   Social Contagion

The process by which an innovation is passed from one tie to another is called *social contagion*. This process is similar in many ways to the spread of an infectious disease. The model, which is a chain-like form, starts with a small number of people who adopt the innovation. This number increases in the second stage when many other people adopt the innovation. Although the number of adopters increases largely in the second stage, the growth rate decreases, particularly after 10–20% of the actors have adopted. In the third stage, the number of people who adopt the innovation decreases until the diffusion process slowly reaches its end.

Those who decide to adopt the innovation are doing so either dependently (i.e., they received information that other people had adopted the innovation) or independently. Those who adopt an innovation dependently are assuming that because others also adopted the innovation, it is a strong signal of its value. The information they receive can be either local (information about the behavior of his or her immediate neighbors, e.g., coworkers in a company) or global (information about the behavior of all the individuals in the extended network, e.g., a union).

The process of adopting an innovation can be represented as a graph called the *diffusion curve*. In this curve, which has the sigmoid function shape (S), the x-axis is the lifetime of a diffusion, and the y-axis is the percentage of innovation adopters.

It should be noted that the size of adoption and adoption speed are bigger in dense networks than in sparse networks, unconnected networks, and networks with cut points or bridges. An individual with a larger number of neighbors is likely to adopt earlier than a person with few neighbors. A diffusion that starts with a person having a central position in the network can be faster than with a person positioned at the network periphery.

8.8   Adoption Rate

The *adoption rate* is a metric used to measure the speed of the diffusion process at a particular time. This metric represents the number of new people who adopt the innovation at a given time. Clearly, network structure has a high impact on the diffusion process such that a diffusion process, which starts with a node in a central position, can reach a significant amount of the desired population in a shorter time. However, the network structure is not the only parameter. The type of innovation itself and personal characteristics of individuals also influence the flow of adoption.

8.9   Adoption Categories and Thresholds

Not everybody can get infected if only his or her neighbor is infected. Friendship alone is not enough to persuade someone to adopt something. This is because some people are less receptive to innovation than other people. One way to explain this observation is through what is called adoption categories.

According to the *adoption categories*, people can be classified based on their adoption time in relevance to all other adopters. For example, in marketing, adopters are categorized into four categories: early adopters, who constitute 16%; early majority, who constitute 34%; late majority, who constitute 34%; and late adopters or laggards, who constitute 16% of all adopters. This type of classification is important for marketers because it helps them identify the social and demographic characteristics of early adopters.

8.10   Amount of Exposure

The *amount of exposure*, for a particular person in a network at a given time, is the portion of a person's neighbors who have adopted the innovation before that time. Once exposure reaches its required level for that person, he or she will approve the

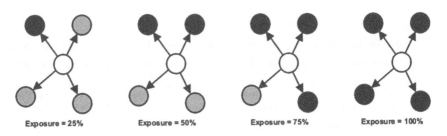

Fig. 8.2 Amount of exposure at four-time steps

innovation and start infecting others. This model treats time more explicitly in the sense that it models what happens at the microlevel at each point in the time during a diffusion. Some researchers refer to the amount of exposure as *network exposure*, referring to the influence of a person's social network and measured with the following equation:

$$E_{i=} \frac{\sum W_{ij} \, y_j}{\sum W_i}$$

where W is the network weight matrix that represents the direct contacts of one person and y is a vector of adoption behavior. In the case of egocentric networks, network exposure model can be weighted by many factors such as the frequency of interaction and the similarity between ego and his or her neighbors. With sociometric data, many types of social influence can be used to weight network exposure model.

Suppose that a person has four friends in his social network. Network exposure (or E_i) is the proportion of those who have adopted an innovation (Fig. 8.2).

The above figure shows network exposure for a person with four friends at four points in time. At the first time point, this person has one adopter, so exposure is 25%. At the second time point, there are two adopters, so network exposure is 50%. At the next time point, there are three adopters so exposure is 75%. After all four friends adopt, exposure is 100%.

Adoption of innovation is not a straightforward process as it depends on a person's characteristics and features of the innovation. Even though some people are not close enough to the source of diffusion, they still adopt early. This is because the amount of exposure varies over time and among people. Knowledge about a friend's adoption or that other persons with similar network positions have adopted may persuade a person to adopt.

For any innovation to be adopted, the expected adopter should be in agreement with the relevance, content, benefit, immediacy, and source of the innovation. This means that innovations should be observable, have a relative advantage over current practices, be compatible with the sociocultural paradigm, and not be highly complex.

It is possible to calculate adoption time for each person at each point in time. This process is called *event history analysis*. This is important because, at the time that we have a diffusion of a new product, we can analyze for each person whether he (or she) has adopted the product and how many of his or her neighbors have adopted it too.

8.11 Adopters and Adoption

People show different levels of exposure before they adopt. For example, some people can be easily persuaded such that they only need to know someone who had already adopted the idea, whereas others would take a longer time to adopt. Also, some people receive more exposure, whether from media or social ties, than others. This is referred to as *threshold of exposure*, which represents the level of exposure that an individual needs to adopt an innovation. Identifying these thresholds (also called *individual tipping points*) is important for researchers because it enables them to understand the different types of adopters and the low- and high-threshold ones.

Early adopters are those who are more vulnerable to innovations such that they will do so when only a few people in the network have already adopted. In other words, their thresholds are low. Such people do no wait for a majority of their network to adopt the innovation before they are willing to. They take risks and adopt new behaviors before their peers are ready to do so.

Late adopters (or *laggards*), on the other hand, are hard to persuade and will only adopt once most others in their network have adopted. They are typically embedded in sparse social networks, have lower social status, are less exposed to mass media, and tend to learn about new ideas or products from interpersonal channels, particularly trusted peers.

People with lower threshold values are more innovative and are expected to adopt an innovation earlier than noninnovative people. We expect that those people turn to the media to learn about new ideas and trends. This occurs because they have few peers to take advice from about the new idea or trend. When the adoption occurs, they transport the new idea or trend to their local community, acting as bridges.

This positive relation between low exposure thresholds and innovativeness (adopting the innovation earlier than other actors in his or her social circle) conditions the presence of extensive media use, many contacts outside the local community, a high level of education, and a high socioeconomic status.

Back to our adoption model, the first adopters cannot be exposed to earlier adopters. Therefore, their thresholds are zero. On the other hand, the last adopters are very likely to be connected to earlier adopters. Therefore their exposure and thresholds are high at the time of adoption.

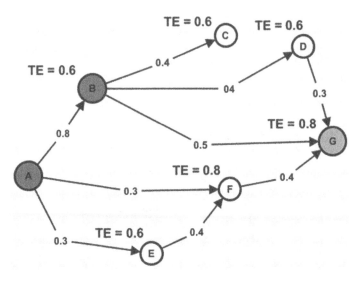

Fig. 8.3 Simple diffusion process

Example

Let us take a look at what a simple diffusion process, which is related to the adoption of innovation in a small network, might look like (Fig. 8.3):

Here is a case where we have the following criteria:

- The network is directed. Nodes (actors) and edges depict the communication channels between actors. A node can only have an effect on the node (or nodes) that it is connected to. Once a node is activated, it can activate its neighboring nodes.
- TE numbers on the chart are the threshold of exposure values, which represents the level of exposure that an individual needs to adopt an innovation. For instance, nodes G and F both have a threshold of exposure equals 0.8. Each of the remaining nodes has a threshold of exposure equals 0.6.
- The numbers on the edges represent the degree of relative influence (network exposure such as trust, persuasion, or blind imitation) one node has on another. For instance, node A, which is the source of the diffusion, has relative influence levels of 0.8, 0.3, and 0.3 on nodes B, F, and E, respectively.
- Node B has already adopted the innovation because the relative influence of node A on node B exceeded the threshold of exposure of node B, which is 0.6.
- Node G is thinking of adopting the innovation. It is receiving an adequate accumulative support from its neighbors that exceeds its threshold of exposure, which is 0.8. Note that knowing that node B has adopted the innovation was not sufficient for node G to adopt the innovation. It needed further support from one of the two remaining nodes before feeling confident enough to make the adoption.
- None of the nodes C, D, E, and F has received the adequate level of influence from its neighbors that satisfied the requirements of its threshold of exposure.

8.12 Critical Mass

A diffusion process may succeed if almost everybody in the target group adopts the innovation. However, it may fail if only a few people adopt and spread the innovation. This observation can by justified by what is called *critical mass*, which represents the minimum number of adopters needed to sustain a diffusion process. Once the critical mass is achieved, it has ongoing momentum that keeps the diffusion going and is hard to reverse.

The critical mass concept (also called *critical level* or *the tipping point*) applies to many phenomena and seems nearly ubiquitous. It explains how opinion leaders have a strong effect on others' behavior where this effect can be scaled up to the national or international level.

However, why this happen? I mean why the critical mass causes the number of adopters to flourish suddenly? The answer to this question has two slots. The first one looks at the process as purely quantitative. When a sufficient number of well-connected people are achieved, other people become exposed to the innovation, after which even more people are exposed. The second slot looks at the process as a qualitative change to the system, namely, a sudden lowering of individual thresholds that makes some people feel confident or even obliged to adopt the innovation.

Betweenness centrality measure is typically linked to critical mass. Targeting those with high betweenness centralities in the network is a good strategy for launching a successful innovation.

The diffusion process requires, in its first stages, outside help in the form of, for example, an advertisement campaign. However, in later stages, the diffusion process can sustain or even accelerate itself without help from outside, particularly when a sufficient number of opinion leaders adopt the innovation. Social contagion then ensures wide and rapid diffusion.

If a diffusion fails to reach the critical mass within a certain amount of time, its adoption rates level off, and the diffusion eventually dies. In contrast, a diffusion may reach its critical mass, and the adoption grows exponentially until it reaches what is called *saturation point*—a point in which almost all those who received the exposure have adopted the innovation. From that point, the diffusion will start to decline and finally dies.

The pinpoint of the moment when critical mass is reached is not easy. We may need to have detailed information about the effects of some events such as media campaigns and social contagions on the diffusion process. Two approaches are proposed by researchers in an attempt to know if a critical mass is reached or not: the first approach uses a rule of thumb and assumes that a particular phenomenon occurs when the innovation has been adopted by 16 (or 10–20) percent of all people who will adopt eventually. The other perspective assumes that a diffusion process attains its critical mass when the most central people have adopted. At that point, so many actors in the network are exposed to adopters, and many of them have achieved their exposure thresholds.

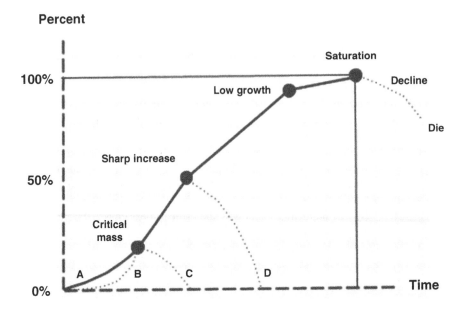

Fig. 8.4 Diffusion curve for the new social media platform

Example

Suppose that we want to draw the diffusion curve for a new social media platform. The website administrators tried to build local marketplace that spans the entire country. They first confined to a small dense local community but expanded later to include all other communities in the country (Fig. 8.4).

The innovation adoption model, shown above, starts with a limited number of people. The x-axis indicates the time of adoption and the y-axis, thresholds, the percentage of network contacts who have adopted. We can see, for example, that 50% of the community had adopted when roughly half the time had passed. We can see, however, that many people have thresholds above and below this value.

Path A shows a rapid and complete adoption by a population. After reaching the required critical mass in the second stage, the number of adopters increases sharply, but the last part of it witnesses a decrease in the growth rate. After reaching saturation in the final stage, the number of adopters decreases, and the diffusion model dies. The curve (growth of population) witnesses what is *fluctuation points*, times where the curve accelerated or deaccelerated dramatically. What happened is that the new social media platform is especially prone to critical mass effects because when this innovation was adopted by a largely sufficient number of people, it became too difficult for them to defect to another medium. Although the adoption curve A shows a simple natural growth of adoption, it does not tell us why some people have adopted the product, why do some people do so much later than others, or why some people never adopt it at all.

Other scenarios are also likely for the product adoption. For example, path B shows a similar pattern to path A but follows a longer lag phase. In path C, the adoption failed to reach the critical mass (which is needed to convince the majority of the audience of the utility of the product), while path D witnesses a sudden decline for an unknown reason although the critical mass threshold is achieved.

Motivations of innovation adoption are quite different before and after a system has reached its critical mass such that adoption before the critical mass carries more risk.

Various types of models have been developed, such as game theoretical, epidemic, threshold, and cascade, to study the information diffusion in social networks. In the following section, we will consider information diffusion in epidemics.

8.13 Epidemics

An epidemic is a disease outbreak such as malaria, bubonic plague, or AIDS that spreads widely via some spreading mechanism such as breathing, blood transfusion, drinking, eating, or sexual activity, within a population of hosts such as humans, animals, or plants. Although the term is commonly used in the context of diseases and their spreading throughout a population, it can also be used to describe the spread of perceived problems in a society or the adoption of a product.

Understanding the potential of an epidemic requires that we fully understand the biological process within each host, the immune system process, interactions among individuals, and social and cultural attributes.

We also need, from a network perspective, to understand the structure of the network and the significance of nodes (persons) within the network. By exposing the structure of the underlying network, it becomes highly possible to gain considerable insight into the potential spread of the diffusion (disease) and whether a new diffusion will succeed or not.

- Highly influential nodes (hubs) in the network enable a rapid spread of a disease through the network. In contrast, poorly connected or periphery nodes would slow the spreading of information and allow only a small portion of the network to get exposed to the diffusion.
- Networks with lots of localized clusters (i.e., a highly fragmented low-density network) may limit the spread of a disease and will have difficulty in establishing any momentum, whereas dense networks with few gaps (i.e., few boundary spanners) would promote the dissemination of the disease.

The transmission of a disease in a network can be stopped via some outside intervention such as simple avoidance, vaccination, or isolation. Such procedures are highly capable of reducing and perhaps halting the spread of the disease.

8.14   Epidemic Models

Epidemic modeling has been an active research area for researchers working on network-based dynamic process models. The Black Death epidemic in the thirteenth century, the Great Plague of London, the smallpox epidemic in the seventeenth century, and recent epidemics such as HIV/AIDS, SARS, and H5N1 motivated the study of epidemics and introduction of the epidemic models.

An epidemic model is a simplified means of describing the transmission of an infectious disease through individuals. Various models have been developed to study the mechanisms by which diseases spread, to predict the future course of various real-world outbreaks, and to evaluate strategies to control an epidemic. In the following section, we will take a look at a group of traditional (i.e., nonnetwork) epidemic models.

8.15   Deterministic Compartmental Models

In the *deterministic compartmental model*, individuals in the population are assigned to different subgroups or compartments such that each represents a specific stage of the epidemic. This model is useful for dealing with large populations, such as in the case of tuberculosis. It categorizes people according to their state on the disease. All people are in one of these three states:

1. Susceptible (S): not infected yet but susceptible to catch the disease
2. Infected (I): caught the disease and contagious
3. Recovered (R): no longer contagious or susceptible to reinfection

A combination of these three letters gives several disease models. The common ones are SIR, SIS, SI, and SIRS. All of these models were originally designed to study how infectious diseases break out and spread over a population. They also describe the disease cycle in a host, using a combination of terms (I, R, S) to characterize each stage. In the following section, we will focus on one of these models, which is the SIR model.

8.16   SIR Model

This *susceptible-infected-recovered (SIR)* model, which was first introduced by Kermack and McKendrick in 1932, describes a disease where a person is susceptible, gets infected, recovers, and becomes finally immune to the disease. This model is the one most commonly used class of the continuous-time epidemic models. Examples of such diseases include polio, measles, mumps, and rubella. In the first phase, people start out to be initially susceptible to the disease. In the second phase,

Fig. 8.5 SIR model
showing the three phases

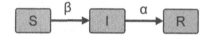

they may become infected by contact with another infected person. They can also infect others in this phase. In the third phase, they become recovered and cannot get infected again.

The SIR model was successfully used on large real-world networks to explore how the structure of the underlying network affects the diffusion process. It was also used to study the information spread taking place in conjoint frameworks. It was also used to explore the spread of violence or extremist topics in social media.

Three components are included in this model: the nodes that are connected to each other, the paths that the disease takes to spread, and the way that these nodes get infected and then recover.

At any time step, only infected nodes can infect any of the neighboring nodes which are in a susceptible state to the disease with some probability β. After that time step, the node that was previously in the infected state moves into a recovered state with probability α and is no longer able to infect others or get infected. Figure 8.5 above depicts the SIR model.

Example
The following figure shows a hypothetical diffusion of the epidemic through a small network consisting of eight nodes. These nodes are connected through symmetric ties that allow for the spread of infection from one node to another. Nodes that get infected can infect others but eventually recover. We are assuming that one infected neighbor is enough to become susceptible to the disease. The figure shows four rounds of diffusion, beginning with two infected nodes, A and B. Each round represents the network status at a given period (Fig. 8.6).

1. Nodes A and B in round 1 have knowledge about the information (i.e., they are infected) and can transmit the information to their neighbors. However, they recover from the infection in the next round. When they recover, they forget all about this information (infection) or lose interest in it. They cannot acquire the same infection for the second time.
2. Nodes C, D, and E do not know yet about the information (infection), but they are susceptible in round 1 due to their connections to the infected nodes, although not infected yet. This does not mean that the infection is inevitable, as many factors will influence whether an exposed person will catch a disease or not. These nodes become infected in round 2, recover in round 3, and never become infected or contagious again.
3. Nodes F, G, and H in round 1 are neither infected nor susceptible. However, they become susceptible in round 2, infected in round 3, and finally recover in round 4.

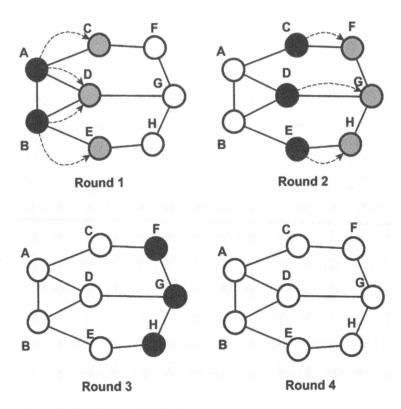

Fig. 8.6 Hypothetical diffusion of epidemic

8.17 Properties of the SIR Model

Some of the properties that we should put in mind regarding the functionality of the SIR model:

- The SIR model puts no consideration to the level of susceptibility or what makes some people more or less likely to catch a disease. This means that a person is either susceptible or not.
- The processes included in this model are deterministic (as opposed to stochastic) which means this model assumes that any susceptible person who is exposed to an infection will get infected too. This assumption is not very realistic in real life because some people are more robust to diseases compared to some others who are genetically more likely to get sick. Also, disease spread at different rates and individuals have various levels of exposure to them.
- The model assumes that after the recovery from a disease, the person will no longer become susceptible. In the susceptible-infected-recover-susceptible (SIRS) model, an individual is susceptible, becomes sick, recovers, enjoys a period of immunity, and finally becomes susceptible again.

- In the SIR model, when a person recovers from a disease, he or she becomes immune to the disease. In contrast, according to the susceptible-infected-susceptible (SIS) model, the infected person does not become immune to the disease after the infection. On the other hand, the susceptible-infected (SI) model describes fatal diseases where the infected person never returns to the recovered or susceptible states.

Example

We will see how we can model epidemic spreading on a network. The following example gives credit to the book.

The network structure influences infection such that nodes with a high degree will potentially infect neighbors and also get infected.

```
In:  # NetworkX for network representation
     import networkx as nx
     # Some handy mathematical functions
     import math
     # Random numbers from numpy
     import numpy as np
     import numpy.random as rnd
     # Important elements of matplotlib
     import matplotlib.pyplot as plt
     import matplotlib.colors as clr
     import matplotlib.cm as cmx
     # Plot all graphics in-line in the notebook
     %matplotlib inline

In:  SPREADING_SUSCEPTIBLE = 'S'
     SPREADING_INFECTED = 'I'
     SPREADING_RECOVERED = 'R'

     def spreading_init( g ):
         """Initialise all node in the graph to be susceptible."""
         for i in g.node.keys():
             er.node[i]['state'] = SPREADING_SUSCEPTIBLE

In:  def spreading_seed( g, pSick ):
         """Inject a random proportion of nodes in the graph."""
         for i in g.node.keys():
             if(rnd.random() <= pSick):
                 er.node[i]['state'] = SPREADING_INFECTED
```

We define a function that, given β and α, makes an SIR model function and returns it for later use:

```
In:    def spreading_make_sir_model( pInfect, pRecover ):
           """Return an SIR model function for given infection and
       recovery probabilities."""

           # model (local rule) function
           def model( g, i ):
               if g.node[i]['state'] == SPREADING_INFECTED:
                   # infect susceptible neighbours with probability
       pInfect
                   for m in g.neighbors(i):
                       if g.node[m]['state'] == SPREADING_SUSCEPTIBLE:
                           if rnd.random() <= pInfect:
                               g.node[m]['state'] = SPREADING_INFECTED

                   # recover with probability pRecover
                   if rnd.random() <= pRecover:
                       g.node[i]['state'] = SPREADING_RECOVERED
           return model
```

Now, we define the spreading process as a function that takes a graph and a model function and applies the model to every node in the graph:

```
In:    def spreading_step( g, model ):
           """Run a single step of the model over the graph."""
           for i in g.node.keys():
               model(g, i)
```

We will also define a function that applies the same model dynamics repeatedly for a number of iterations:

```
In:    def spreading_run( g, model, iter ):
           """Run a number of iterations of the model over the graph."""
           for i in xrange(iter):
               spreading_step(g, model)
```

Now, we create the model. We will use the Erdos-Renyi ER model:

```
In:    n = 1000
       er = nx.erdos_renyi_graph(n, 0.01)
```

We will visualize the model using the spring layout (Fig. 8.7).

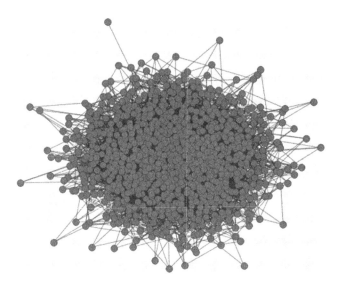

Fig. 8.7 Epidemic spreading on a network

```
In:   fig = plt.figure(figsize=(10, 8))

      # some visual styling for the figure
      ax = fig.gca()
      ax.grid(False)                    # no grid
      ax.get_xaxis().set_ticks([])   # no ticks on the axes
      ax.get_yaxis().set_ticks([])
      # run the spring layout algorithm over the network
      pos = nx.spring_layout(er, iterations = 50, k = 2/math.sqrt(n))

      # draw the network using the computed positions for the nodes
      nx.draw_networkx_edges(er, pos, width = 1, alpha = 0.4)
      nx.draw_networkx_nodes(er, pos, node_size=100, alpha = 1,
      linewidths = 0.5)
      plt.show()
```

```
Out:
```

We then network the model with a certain proportion of sick individuals, with the rest being susceptible:

```
In:    # initialise with 5% sick people
       spreading_init(er)
       spreading_seed(er, 0.05)
```

Finally, we create the network dynamics:

```
In:      # SIR model with 30% infection rate and 10% recovery rate
         model = spreading_make_sir_model(0.3, 0.05)
```

We now run the model:

```
In:      # run SIR model dynamics over the network
         spreading_run(er, model, 100)
```

We can also inquire what percentage of the model is infected:

```
In:      infected = [ v for (v, attr) in er.nodes(data = True) if
         attr['state'] == SPREADING_RECOVERED ]
         print float(len(infected)) / n
```

```
Out:     0.994
```

Appendices

Appendix A: Python 3.x Quick Syntax Guide

Python is a general-purpose and multi-paradigm dynamic object-oriented programming language. Named for the British comedy group *Monty Python*, Python is a simple, portable, open-source, and powerful programming language that allows to work quickly and integrate more efficiently.

The first version of Python code (0.9.0) was published by Guido van Rossum in February 1991 at the CWI (Centrum Wiskunde & Informatica) in the Netherlands, Amsterdam. It was derived from ABC programming language, which is a general-purpose programming language that had been developed at the CWI. Although today Python is maintained by a core development team at the institute, van Rossum still holds a vital role in directing its progress.

Python can be described as (i) an interpreted language, which means it is processed at runtime by the interpreter; (ii) interactive, which means it is possible to use Python prompt to interact directly with the interpreter; (iii) object-oriented-based language; and (iv) a beginner's language, which means it is a great option for beginner programmers who want to develop applications.

Python has many uses. For example, it is used for (i) Web development → Django, TurboGears, and Plone; (ii) communicating with databases → MongoDB, MySQL, PostgreSQL, and Oracle; (iii) desktop GUI → GTK+, QT, Tk, etc.; (iv) scientific computing → SciPy, Scientific Python, etc.; (iv) network programming → Twisted; (vi) software development → SCons, Buildbot, Roundup, etc; and (vii) games and 3D graphics → PyGame, PyKyra, etc.

One of Python's greatest strengths is the size and scope of its standard library and the other open-source libraries such as libraries used for mathematical functions, scientific computations, graphics, machine learning, XML parsing, downloading Web pages, etc. In fact, designing a small core language with a large and extensible standard library was the idea of van Rossum at the very beginning.

M.Z. Al-Taie, S. Kadry, *Python for Graph and Network Analysis*, Advanced Information and Knowledge Processing, DOI 10.1007/978-3-319-53004-8

Everything in Python is represented as an object (e.g., integers, lists, strings, functions, modules, classes, etc.) or by relations between objects such that each object gets an identity, a type, and a value. Although Python is object oriented and everything in the language is an object, it also supports procedural, functional, aspect-oriented, design-by-contract, and logic programming styles of programming. This is useful when implementing machine learning algorithms as it allows for the use of the most suitable programming style for each case.

Python differs from other high-level languages (e.g., C, C++, or Java) in that the code written in dynamically typed languages such as Python tends to be shorter than in C, C++, or Java. In Python, no pointers are used, and no prior compilation to bytecode is required as it can be directly interpreted.

Python Syntax

- Python files have extension .py.
- Indentation is used instead of braces in Python to delimit blocks. The number of spaces is variable, but all statements within the same block must be indented the same amount.
- Basic data types: numbers (i.e., *integer*, float, and complex), Boolean, and sequences (i.e., strings, lists, dictionaries, and tuples).
- The header line for compound statements, such as if, while, def, and class, should be terminated with a colon (:).
- The semicolon (;) is optional at the end of the statement.
- print is a keyword for giving output to a console or a file. For example, print("Hello Python!").
- Reading from keyboard: name = input("enter your name"). The method returns a line of user input as a string.
- Comments: single-line comment (#) and multiple-line comments ("'____"'").
- help(<obj>) provides help/documentation for the object using pydoc.help.
- dir(<obj>) lists the attributes/methods available for that object. Attributes/methods starting with "/" are internal attributes/methods and should not be used unless you know what you are doing. dir() returns names in current scope

Variables

- No prior type declaration is required for variables.
- A variable can refer to any data type (like Tuple, List, Dictionary, Int, String, Complex, or any other object). They are references to allocated memory.
- Python is dynamically typed. The declaration happens automatically when the value is assigned to a variable.
- Variables can change type, simply by assigning them a new value of a different type.

- Python allows assigning a single value to several variables simultaneously.
- It is also possible to assign multiple objects to multiple variables.

Numbers

- Numbers in Python are immutable objects. Immutable means that objects cannot change their values, for example, 1234, 3.1415, 3+4j.
- The three built-in data types for numbers in Python 3 are (i) integers, (ii) floating-point numbers, and (iii) complex numbers that consist of two parts: real and imaginary.
- Common number functions include int(x), float(x), abs(x), exp(x), log(x), pow(x,y), and sqrt(x).

Strings

- A contiguous set of characters in between quotation marks, for example, mystr = "This is a quick Python 3.x syntax guide."
- Python strings are immutable objects (i.e., cannot change their values).
- There is no "character" data type in python.
- To update an existing string, we can (re)assign a variable to another string.
- Strings of length one character are treated as normal strings (i.e., no type *character* is used in Python syntax).
- Single ('), double ("), and triple (""" or """""") quotes are used to denote strings.
- String indexes start at **0** and work their way from **−1** at the end.
- Common string operators include (+) for concatenation, (*) for repetition, ([ ]) for slicing, ([:]) for range slicing, and (in) to check membership.
- Special characters can be inserted by using the escape character "\".
- Common string methods include str.count(sub, beg=0, end=len(str)), str.isalpha(), str.isdigit(), str.lower(), str.upper(), str.replace(old, new), str.split(str = ' '), str.strip(), and str.title().
- Common string functions include str(x) to convert x to a string and len(string) to find the total length of the string.

Lists

- A list is an ordered group of items or elements. List elements do not have to be of the same type. There can have nesting of lists one inside the other.
- A list contains items separated by commas and enclosed in square brackets, for example, myList = [1, [2, 'three'], 4].

- Python lists are mutable objects which means that they *can* change their values.
- List indexes like strings start at 0 and work their way from −1 at the end. They can be extended at right end.
- Lists can have sublists as elements, and these sublists may contain other sublists.
- List operations include slicing ([ ] and [:]), concatenation (+), repetition (*), and membership (in).
- Common list functions include len(list), max(list), min(list), and list(tuple).
- Common list methods include list.append(obj), list.insert(index, obj), list.count(obj), list.index(obj), list.remove(obj), list.sort(), list.reverse(), and list.pop().

Tuples

- A tuple is an immutable ordered sequence of items. Immutable means cannot be changed once it has been declared. Tuples can be considered as a constant array.
- A tuple contains items separated by commas and enclosed in parentheses, for example, myTuple = (1, 'spam', 4, 'U'). There can have nesting of tuples one inside the other.
- A tuple can be updated by (re)assigning a variable to another tuple.
- Tuples are preferred over lists in use if we want faster processing and we want to protect data against accidental changes.
- Tuple operations include slicing ([ ] and [:]), concatenation (+), repetition (*), and membership (in).
- A tuple with a single value must include a comma, e.g., t = (17,).

Dictionaries

- Dictionaries are containers which store items in key/value pairs.
- Python dictionaries are mutable objects that can change their values.
- They are kinds of hash table type which consist of key/value pairs of unordered elements. Keys must be immutable data types, usually numbers or strings, and values can be any arbitrary Python object.
- A dictionary is enclosed by curly braces ({ }), the items are separated by commas, and each key is separated from its value by a colon (:), for eample, {'food': 'spam', 'taste': 'yum'}.
- Dictionary's values can be assigned and accessed using square braces ([]) with a key to obtain its value.
- Common dictionary methods include dict.keys(), dict.values(), dict.items(), dict.get(key, default = None), dict.has_key(key), dict.update(dict2), and dict.clear().
- To iterate over dictionary: for key, value in a_dictionary.items(): print key, value.

Conditionals

- If statements are powerful decision-making statements. They are used to control the flow of execution of program. Syntax: [if expression: statement(s)], [if expression: statement(s); else: statement(s)], [if expression1: statement(s); elif expression2: statement(s); else: statement(s)].
- True and False are Boolean objects of class "bool" and they are immutable.
- Python assumes any non-zero and non-null values as True. Otherwise it is False value.
- Python does not provide switch or case statements.

Loops

- Looping is the process of repeatedly executing a block of statements.
- The for loop. It iterates through a list of values. Example: [for x in X: print("current letter is :", x)]. In Python, the for loops may have the optional "else" clause.
- The while loop: while is used for repeated execution of a block of code till a condition holds true. Syntax: [while condition: statement(s)].
- The while-else clause. The optional else clause runs only if the loop exits normally (not by the break). Syntax: while condition: statement(s); else: statement(s).
- Loop control statements: (i) *break*, terminates the loop statement and transfers execution to the statement that comes immediately after the loop; (ii) *continue*, causes the loop to skip the remainder of its body and retest its condition; and (iii) *pass*, used when a statement is required syntactically but we do not want any command or code to be executed.
- range(N) generates a list of numbers [0, 1, ..., N-1], for example, range(i, j, k) where "i" is the start, "j" is the stop condition, and "k" is the step condition.
- List comprehensions. Normal use of \for" loop is to iterate and build a new list. List comprehensions simplify the above task. Syntax: [<expression> for <target> in <iterable> <condiction>].

Python Functions

- A function is a group of statements that executes on request. Syntax: def function_name(parameters):   "function_docstring";   function_statements;   return [expression].
- In Python functions are also objects. Function return type is not required. If the function does not return any value, default value of None is returned. A function can take another function name as an argument and return a function name (as in functional programming languages).

- A function is defined using the keyword *def* followed by function name and parameters.
- Basic types of functions: built-in functions, e.g., dir(), len(), and abs(), and user-defined functions created with the "def" keyword.
- Four types of argument are used with Python functions:

  (i) Required arguments, where arguments are passed to the function in the correct positional order
  (ii) Keyword argument, where Python function call can identify the arguments by the parameter name
  (iii) Default arguments, where the argument has a default value in the function declaration. The default value is used when no value is provided in the function call.
  (iv) Variable-length arguments are used when we want to process unspecified additional argument. An asterisk (*) is used before the variable name.

- It is recommended that all functions have documentation along with the function definition.

File Handling

- Python's *file* is a built-in type in Python. It allows access to files in an operating system-independent manner.
- *File opening.* For file opening, the following expression is used fileObject = open(file_name [, access_mode][, buffering]).
- Common access modes include "r" to open a file for reading only, "w" to open a file for writing only, "a" to open a file for appending, "r+" to open a file for reading and writing, "w+" to open a file for writing and reading, "a+" to open a file for reading and writing where new data is added at the end, and "b" to open a file in binary mode.
- *Closing a file.* To close a file in Python, use fileObject.close(). The close() method flushes any unwritten data and closes the file object. The method is used when the program does not need the file anymore.
- *File renaming and deleting.* Python "os" module provides methods to rename and delete files, for example, import os; os.rename("old_name.txt", "new_name.txt") or os.remove(file_name).
- *Reading a File.* To read a file, you can use fileObject.read([count]). Different formats for reading: the read() method reads the whole file at once, the readline() method reads one line each time from the file, and the readlines() method reads all lines from the file in a list.
- *Writing in a File.* The write() method writes any string in a file. The file should be open.

Exception Handling

- Common exceptions in Python: NameError-TypeError-IndexError-KeyError-Exception.
- An empty except statement can catch any exception.
- *Finally*, clause is always executed before finishing try statements.

Modules

- A module is a file with Python code that contains definitions for functions, classes, and variables. They help to group related code for better code understanding.
- Any python file (.py) can work as a module. If the file is written to execute when invoked, it is executed when imported.
- Modules can be executed by using the *import* statement, for example, import module1, module2, module3, etc.
- Python's *from* statement can be used to import specific attributes from a module, for example, from module1 import name1, name3, name3, etc.
- *import* * statement can be used to import all names from a module, for example, from module1 import *.

Classes

- A class is a set of attributes that characterize any object of the class.
- The attributes are data members (class variables and instance variables) and methods.
- Constructor method: first method *__init__*() is called the class constructor or initialization method that Python calls when a new instance of this class is created.
- Creating classes: class class_name: class_body.
- Creating objects: obj1 = class_name().

Appendix B: NetworkX Tutorial

NetworkX is a Python language software package and an open-source tool for the creation, manipulation, and study of the structure, dynamics, and functions of complex networks. *Complex* networks are networks with nontrivial topological features—features that do not occur in simple networks such as lattices or random graphs but often occur in real graphs, e.g., circadian rhythms, electrochemical reactions, laser arrays, neuron networks, Josephson junction arrays, etc.

NetworkX can load, store, and analyze networks, generate new networks, build network models, and draw networks. It is a computational network modeling tool and not a software tool development. The first public release of the library, which is all based on Python, was in April 2005. The library can engage with languages other than Python such as C, C++, and FORTRAN.

The library is implemented as a dictionary of dictionaries with a node-centric view of the network that is based on nodes and connections between them. Nodes can be any hashable object such as a text string, an image, an XML object, another Graph, a customized node object, etc. Python's none object should not be used as a node as it determines whether optional function arguments have been assigned in many functions.

Each graph, node, and edge can hold key/value attribute pairs (e.g., weights, labels, and colors) in an associated attribute dictionary (the keys must be hashable). Edges are represented as tuples with optional edge data and can hold arbitrary data (e.g., weights, time series, etc.).

Although NetworkX is not ideal for large-scale problems with fast-processing requirements, it is a great option for real-world network analysis:

- Most of the core algorithms rely on extremely fast legacy code.
- It uses standard graph algorithms.
- It has an extensive set of native readable and writable formats.
- It is easy to install and use on major platforms with a strong online up-to-date documentation.
- It is ideal for representing networks of different types like, e.g., classic graphs, random graphs, and synthetic networks.
- It takes advantage of Python's ability to import data from outer sources.
- NetworkX includes many graph generator functions and facilities to read and write graphs in many formats such as .edgelist, .adjlist, .gml, .graphml, .pajek, etc.

NetworkX was not designed as a graph drawing package. However, it provides basic drawing capabilities through matplotlib. For more complex visualization techniques, it is preferred to use the open-source Graphviz software package (NetworkX provides an interface to that package). Also, the drawing package in NetworkX is not yet compatible with Python versions 3.0 and above.

Graph Types

```
>>> Import networkx as nx          # import library
```
–   To create an empty graph with no nodes or edges:
```
>>> G = nx.Graph()                 # create new simple undirected graphs
>>> EG = nx.empty_graph(100)       # create an empty graph
>>> DG = nx.DiGraph                # create a simple directed graphs
>>> MG = nx.MultiGraph()           # create undirected with parallel edges
>>> MDG = nx.MultiDiGraph()        # create directed with parallel edges
>>> CG = nx.complete_graph(10)     # create a complete graph
>>> PG = nx.path_graph(5)          # create a chain of nodes
>>> CBG = nx.complete_bipartite_graph(n1, n2)    # create bipartite
>>> GG = nx.grid_graph([10, 10, 10, 10])    # arbitrary dimensional lattice
```

–   To get graph attributes
```
>>> G.graph
```
–   To convert to undirected
```
>>> G.to_undirected()
```
–   To convert to directed
```
>>> G.to_directed()
```
–   To clear a graph from nodes and edges
```
>>> G.clear()
```

Nodes

–   To add one node at a time:
```
>>> G.add_node(1)
```
–   To add a list of nodes:
```
>>> G.add_nodes_from([3, 4, 5])    # takes any iterable collection
```
–   To add nbunch of nodes:
```
>>> H = nx.path_graph(10)
>>> G.add_nodes_from(H)
```
–   To add a graph as a node
```
>>> G.add_node(H)
```
–   To print the number of nodes
```
>>> G.number_of_nodes()
```
–   To print graph nodes
```
>>> G.nodes()
```
–   To print type of nodes
```
>>> type(G.nodes())                # it will show class list
```
–   To relabel nodes
```
>>> nx.relabel_nodes(G, mapping, copy = True)    # mapping → new labels
```
–   To check node membership
```
>>> G.has_node(1)
```

Edges

- To add an edge
        >>> G.add_edge(1, 2)
- To add a list of edges
        >>> G.add_edges_from([6, 7])   # automatically add those nodes
- To add edges from a list
        >>> edge = ("a", "b")
        >>> G.add_edge(*edge)
- To check edge membership
        >>> G.has_edge("a", "b")
- To print the number of edges
        >>> G.number_of_edges()
- To remove an edge
        >>> G.remove_edge(1, 2)
- To remove a list of edges
        >>> G.remove_edges_from([(1, 2), (3, 4)])
- To print graph edges
        >>> G.edges()
- General read format
        >>> nx.read_format("path/to/file.txt",...options...)
- To read edge list from file
        >>> el = nx.read_edgelist("test.edges", comments = "#")
- To read adjacency list from file
        >>> al = nx.read_adjlist("test2.adj")
- General write format
        >>> nx.write_format(g,"path/to/file.txt",...options...)
- To write edge list
        >>> nx.write_edgelist(G, "newFile.edges", comments = "#", data = True)
- To print type of edges
        >>> type(G.edges())   # it will show class list

Directed Graphs

– To create an empty directed graph
>>> DG = nx.DiGraph()   # creates simple directed graphs
– To add weighted edges to DG
>>> DG.add_weighted_edges_from([(1, 2, 2.7), (3, 1, 0.5)])
– To calculate outdegree
>>> DG.out_degree()
– To calculate outdegree with attributes included
>>> DG.out_degree(with_labels = True)   # Boolean should be capitalized
– To calculate successors
>>> DG.successors(1)
– To calculate predecessors
>>> DG.predecessors(1)
– To calculate neighbors
>>> DG.neighbors(1)
– To convert directed graphs to undirected
>>> DG.to_undirected()

Attributed Graphs

– To add attributes
>>> G = nx.Graph(day = "Wednesday")
– To update attributes
>>> G.graph["day"] = "Thursday"
– To add attributes to nodes
>>> G.add_node(1, time = "5am")   # attributes are optional
>>> G.add_nodes_from([3], time = "2am")
– To get node attributes
>>> G.node[1]
– To add attributes to edges
>>> G.add_edges_from([(1, 2), (3, 4)], color = "blue")
– To get edge attributes
>>> G[1][2]
– To get a particular attribute value
>>> G[1][2]["color"]

Weighted Graphs

– To add weighted edges to a graph
>>> G.add_edge(1, 2, weight = 3.3)
>>> G.add_edge(3, 4, weight = 4.3)
– To calculate node degree without weight
>>> G.degree(1)
– To calculate node degree with weight included
>>> G.degree(1, weight = "weight")
– To calculate all node degrees
>>> G.degree(weight = "weight")

Multigraphs

– To build a multigraph
>>> MG = nx.MultiGraph()
– To add edges to MG
>>> MG.add_weighted_edges_from([1, 2, 0.75), (1, 2, 1,25), (2, 3, 0.75)])
– To calculate degrees
>>> MG.degree(weight = "weight")

Classic Graph Operations

>>> nx.subgraph(G, nbunch)   # induce subgraph of G on nodes in
nbunch
>>> nx.union(G1, G2)   # graph union
>>> nx.disjoint_union(G1, G2)   # graph union/all node are different
>>> nx.cartesian_product(G1, G2)   # return Cartesian product graph
>>> nx.compose(G1, G2)   # combine graphs identifying common nodes
>>> nx.complement(G)   # graph complement
>>> nx.create_empty_graph(G)   # return an empty copy of the same
graph class
>>> nx.convert_to_undirected(G)   # return an undirected copy of G
>>> nx.convert_to_directed(G)   # return a directed copy of G

Graph Generators

```
# Using a call to one of the classic small graphs
>>> petersen = nx.petersen_graph()
>>> tutte = nx.tutte_graph()
>>> maze = nx.sedgewick_maze_graph()
>>> tet = nx.tetrahedral_graph()
# Using a (constructive) generator for a classic graph
>>> k_5 = nx.complete_graphs(10)
>>> k_3_5 = nx.complete_bipartite_graph(3, 5)
>>> barbell = nx.barbell_graph(15, 15)
>>> lollipop = nx.lollipop_graph(5, 10)
# Using a stochastic graph generator
>>> er = nx.erdos_renyi_graph(50, 0.5)
>>> ws = nx.watts_strogatz_graph(20, 2, 0.5)
>>> ba = nx.barabasi_albert_graph(50, 5)
>>> red = nx.random_lobster(100, 0.9, 0.9)
```

Basic Network Analysis

– To find connected components
  >>> nx.connected_components(G)
– To sort nodes based on node degree
  >>> sorted(nx.degree(G).values())
– To calculate degree of a specific node
  >>> G.degree(1)
– To calculate all degrees
  >>> G.degree()
– To see if network is connected
  >>> nx.is_connected(G)
– To calculate network global clustering coefficient
  >>> nx.clustering(G)
– To calculate the clustering coefficient of each node
  >>> nx.clustering(G, with_labels = True)
– To calculate coefficient for a particular node
  >>> nx.clustering(G, 1)
– To find the shortest path between two nodes
  >>> nx.shortest_path(G, 1, 3)
– To find the length of the shortest path between two nodes
  >>> nx.shortest_path_length(G, 3, 1)
– To find in-degree distribution of G
  >>> G.in_degree()
– To find out-degree distribution of G
  >>> G.out_degree()
– To calculate number of nodes
  >>> G.order()
  >>> nx.number_of_nodes(G)
  >>> len(G)
– To calculate number of edges
  >>> G.size()
  >>> nx.number_of_edges(G)
– To find network diameter
  >>> nx.diameter(G)
– To find network radius
  >>> nx.radius(G)
– To find cores in network
  >>> nx.find_cores(G)

Centrality Measures

- To calculate degree centrality
        >>> nx.degree_centrality(G)
- To calculate betweenness centrality
        >>> nx.betweenness_centrality(G)
- To calculate closeness centrality
        >>> nx.closeness_centrality(G)
- To calculate eigenvector centrality
        >>> nx.eigenvector_centrality(G)

Drawing Graphs

        >>> import matplotlib.pyplot as plt   # Can use GraphViz
- To clear the previous graph
        >>> plt.clf()
- To draw a graph
        >>> nx.draw(G)
        >>> nx.draw_random(G)
        >>> nx.draw_circular(G)
        >>> nx.draw_spectral(G)
- To show the graph
        >>> plt.show()   # to show the file
- To save the graph
        >>> plt.savefig("myFig.png")   # save as png file
- To close the file
        >>> plt.close()
- To extract the main connected component from G
        >>> nx.connected_component_subgraphs(G)   # graph should be
        undirected

Algorithms Package (NetworkX Algorithms)

- Bipartite
- Block
- Boundary
- Centrality (package)
- Clique
- Cluster
- Components (package)

- Core
- Cycles
- Dag
- Distance measures
- Ow (package)
- Isolates
- Isomorphism (package)
- Link analysis (package)
- Matching
- Mixing
- MST
- Operators
- Shortest paths (package)
- Smetric

Reading and Writing

- Adjacency list
- Multiline adjacency list
- Edge list
- GEXF
- GML
- Pickle
- GraphML
- LEDA
- YAML
- SparseGraph6
- Pajek
- GIS shapefile

References

Borgatti SP, Foster PC (2003) The network paradigm in organizational research: A review and typology. J Manag 29(6):991–1013

Fortunato S (2010) Community detection in graphs. Phys Rep 486(3):75–174

Freeman LC (2004) The development of social network analysis: a study in the sociology of science. BookSurge, LLC, South Carolina

Marin A, Wellman B (2010) Social network analysis: an introduction. In: Carrington P, Scott J (eds) Handbook of social network analysis. SAGE Publications

Wasserman S, Faust K (1994) Social network analysis: methods and applications. Cambridge University Press, Cambridge

Bibliography

Abdesslem FB, Parris I, Henderson T (2011) Reliable online social network data collection. In: Abraham A, Hassanien AE (eds) Computational social networks: mining and visualization. Springer, London

Abraham J, Hassanien AE, Snasel V (eds) (2010) Computational social network analysis: trends, tools and research advances. Springer, London

Alhajj R, Rokne J (2014) Encyclopedia of social network analysis and mining. Springer Publishing Company, Incorporated, New York

Al-Taie M, Kadry S (2012) Applying social network analysis to analyze a web-based community. Int J Adv Comput Sci Appl (IJACSA) 3(2):29–41

Al-Taie MZ, Shamsuddin SM, Ahmad NB (2014) Flight MH370 community structure. Int J Adv Soft Comput Appl 6(2)

Barthélemy M (2011) Spatial networks. Phys Rep 499(1):1–101

Berger-Wolf T, Fischhoff I, Rubenstein DI, Sundaresan SR, Tantipathananandh C (2010) Dynamic analysis of social networks of equids. In: Applications of social network analysis ASNA, Zurich

Bohn J, Feinerer I, Hornik K, Mair P (2011) Content-based social network analysis on mailing lists. R J 3(1):11–18

Borgatti SP, Halgin D (2011) Analyzing affiliation networks. In: Carrington P, Scott J (eds) Handbook of social network analysis. SAGE Publications, London

Boschetti A, Massaron L (2015) Python data science essentials. Packt Publishing Ltd., Birmingham

© Springer International Publishing AG 2017
M.Z. Al-Taie, S. Kadry, *Python for Graph and Network Analysis*, Advanced
Information and Knowledge Processing, DOI 10.1007/978-3-319-53004-8

Ojeda T, Murphy SP, Bengfort B, Dasgupta A (2014) Practical data science cookbook. Packt Publishing Ltd., Birmingham

Carrington PJ, Scott J, Wasserman S (eds) (2005) Models and methods in social network analysis. Cambridge University Press, New York

De Nooy W (2003) Social network analysis, graph theoretical approaches to. In: Meyers RA (ed) Springer encyclopedia of complexity and system science, pp 8231–8245

De Nooy W, Mrvar A, Batagelj V (2005) Exploratory social network analysis with Pajek. Cambridge University Press, New York

Dobson S. Complex networks, complex processes, 2016

Easley D, Kleinberg J (2010) Networks, crowds, and markets: reasoning about a highly connected world. Cambridge University Press, New York

Ereteo G, Buffa M, Gandon F, Grohan P, Leitzelman M, Sander P (2008) A state of the art on the social network analysis and its applications on a semantic web. Social Data on the Web (SDoW2008)

Giuffre K (2013) Communities and networks: using social network analysis to rethink urban and community studies. Wiley

Greenhalgh T, Robert G, Bate P, Macfarlane F, Kyriakidou O (2008) Diffusion of innovations in health service organisations: a systematic literature review. Wiley

Hamasaki M, Matsuo Y, Ishida K, Hope T, Nishimura T, Takeda H (2006) An integrated method for social network extraction. In: Proceedings of the 15th international conference on World Wide Web

Huang B, Jebara T (2010) Exact graph structure estimation with degree priors. International conference on machine learning and applications, pp 111–118

Jeong H et al (2001) Lethality and centrality in protein networks. Nature 411(6833):41–42

Kadry, S, Al-Taie, M. Z (2014). Social network analysis: An introduction with an extensive implementation to a large-scale online network using Pajek.

Lappas T, Liu K, Terzi E (2009) Finding a Team of Experts in Social Network. KDD '09 proceedings of the 15th ACM SIGKDD international conference on knowledge discovery and data mining, pp 467–476

Newman MEJ, Lusseau D (2004) Identifying the role that individual animals play in their social network. Proc R Soc London B (Suppl) 271:S477–S481

Newman MEJ (2010) Networks: an introduction. Oxford University Press, New York

Page L, et al. The PageRank citation ranking: bringing order to the web. 1999.

Regan E (2009) Networks: structure and dynamics. In: Meyers RA, editor in chief. Encyclopedia of complexity and system science. Springer; 2009. ISBN-13: 978–0–387-75888-6

Ricci F, Rokach L, Shapira B, Kantor PB (eds) (2011) Recommender systems handbook. Springer, New York

Russell M. A (2013) Mining the Social Web: Data Mining Facebook, Twitter, LinkedIn, Google+, GitHub, and More. O'Reilly Media, Inc.

Sayama H (2015) Introduction to the modeling and analysis of complex systems. Open SUNY Textbooks, Milne Library, Geneseo

Scott J (2000) Social network analysis: a handbook, 2nd edn. SAGE publications, Ltd, London

Serrat O (2009) Social network analysis. Asian Development Bank ADB

Shapira B et al (2011) Recommender systems handbook. Springer, New York

Steen MV (2010) Graph theory and complex networks: an introduction. Published by Maarten Van Steen

Stockman F. N (2004) What binds us when with whom? Content and structures in social network analysis. Extended version of keynote at the SUNBELT XXIV. International social network conference, Portoroz (Slovenia)

Sun H, Peng Y, Chen J, Liu C, Sun Y (2011) A new similarity measure based on adjusted Euclidean distance for memory-based collaborative filtering. J Softw 6(6)

Tang L, Liu H (2010) Graph mining applications to social network analysis. The Kluwer Int Ser Adv Database Syst 40:487–513

Thomas FN, Verlag V (2008) Why context matters: applications of social network analysis

Tsvetovat M, Kouznetsov A (2011) Social network analysis for startups. O'Reilly Media, Inc., California

Valente TW (2010) Social networks and health: Models, methods and applications. Oxford University Press, New York

Wey T, Blumstein D, Shen W, Jordan F (2008) Social network analysis of animal behavior: a promising tool for the study of sociality. Animal Behav 75(2):333–344

Zafarani R, Abbasi MA, Liu H (2014) Social media mining: an introduction. Cambridge University Press, New York

Printed in the United States
By Bookmasters